SOUTH WEST AFRICA

The Last Pioneer Country

by

THOMAS MOLNAR

FLEET PUBLISHING CORPORATION

NEW YORK

TO THE MEMORY OF MY MOTHER

CONTENTS

PART ONE

The Evidence

CHAPTER 1

A HARDLY-KNOWN LAND

ALL OF US have seen maps of a continent projected on the movie screen, then the camera zeroing in on a narrow point; suddenly the map opens up and there appears the land with its vegetation, animals, buildings, roads, and people. The abstract outlines have turned into real life. A superficial floating curiosity has focused on a concrete situation and become involved in the intricacies of a thousand events. Travel has always given me a similar sensation: Arriving at a never-yet-seen spot naturally I cannot help bringing with me recent experiences. But they become instantly obsolete, so strong are the fresh impressions, the new circumstances eager to involve me and intent on crowding out the past.

When I first landed on the territory of South West Africa, I was almost a seasoned traveler on that continent; I had seen more than half of its old and new countries, I had crossed it in several directions. I had even published a book about it, a book I called *Africa: A Political Travel-*

ogue. Yet South West Africa represented something entirely new and fresh; the stories and tales I had heard of this land suggested that it was even more strange and desolate than most of the African land mass; that it was primitive even by African standards; that it was almost *empty* since only some half a million people inhabit its wastelands, big as France and Spain combined.

But the names of its places sang like strange exotic musical phrases, not yet familiar to world press and radio; Katima Molilo on a bend of the Zambesi River; the Skeleton Coast with the shipwrecks of centuries washed ashore; Swakopmund, a German settlement of pre-World War times; the Namib Desert, a strip of sand-dunes running parallel to the ocean for a thousand miles; Oranjemund, where every day half a million dollars worth of diamonds are picked up from the sand among the pebbles.

South West Africa is put down in geography books as a mostly desert-like territory between the Republic of South Africa and Portuguese Angola, with the Kalahari Desert locking it in from the east, and the Atlantic Ocean from the west. It is almost of rectangular shape, but at the northeastern corner it extends a finger, the Caprivi Zipfel, into the heart of south central Africa, establishing a link with Katanga, Zambia, and Rhodesia. And here is where the traveler's surprise begins. According to the bird's-eye view, South West Africa is one of the continent's poorest parts. One expects to see only sand and rocks, a small and miserable population eking out a hard existence, life concentrated in a few small coastal fishing towns. The mere data of demography are not promising either; only some five hundred thousand blacks and eighty thousand whites live here. One almost expects to meet more ghosts among the wrecks of Skeleton Coast and the ruins of old German forts than live men and women.

Yet, once there, both present and past capture the imagination and fasten to the soul as only in few countries. First of all let us look at the past, remote as well as recent. This far corner of the earth has an amazingly agitated history, full of epic adventures of discovery, and bloody tribal wars of extermination. Its recorded history began with the Portuguese, whose landing is commemorated by the Cross of Bartholomeu Dias, near Luderitz, on a rocky promontory furiously assailed by the waves. As Englishmen, South Africans, Swedes, Germans, and Finns tried their fortunes, they left varied mementos: whaling stations, missions, fortresses—and also learned books as their signatures in this near no-man's-land early chronicle.

The chronicle is rich in passion, bloodshed, enslavement, wily tricks, cattle raids, and rebellions. South West Africa's nineteenth century, about which excellent books have been written, is as full of conflict and war as the same period in European or South American history. Black men are no more peaceful and no less intent on conquest, pillage, and genocide than the white men, or men of any other color and race. From a distance, we are tempted to think of South West African tribes as forming one black nation, a scene, perhaps, of internal rivalries, but in basic agreement on their overall interests. This view reflects the western white man's concepts: Just as he is hard put to distinguish the faces of black men from one another, similarly, in his intellectual laziness, he prefers to label Ovambo, Herero, Bergdamara, Nama, Rehoboth Baster, perhaps even Bushmen, as the "South West African nation."

Yet the recent history and present attitudes of these tribes show as much disparity and opposition as that of nations everywhere. Only animal species can be expected to behave alike and graze indifferently side by side when hunger does not torment them; large human groups are distinguished by specific traditions, social structure, past memories, future interests. Differences, even antagonisms are the rule, not the exception among them. The tribes of South West Africa can be just as hostile to each other as French and German, British and Irish, or elsewhere in Africa, those within Nigeria and the Congo. In the last two cases, the decolonizing white man made the, to him, comfortable, but otherwise tragic, error of leaving the heterogeneous groups in one national framework, within the same borders. The accent was on rapid departure; little resistance was offered in London, Paris, or Brussels to the loudest pressure group which promised to forge a *nation* out of very diverse elements, but which in reality planned to set up its own dictatorial rule.

Such were my reflections when I set foot on the soil of South West Africa one day in 1966. These reflections were called forth by newspaper reports at that time about horrible events in Nigeria. I did not doubt that there was a parallel between those events and the past (and potential future) of the territory where I landed, whose history was known to me, although only through reading.

Nigeria had been called the "most hopeful" emerging African state because in its vast territory, tribal groups of vastly different ethnic, religious, and economic structure displayed for a few years attitudes promising a fruitful coexistence. Nigeria was indeed the showpiece of the British (after their hopes had been crushed by Ghana's bloody and squandering dictator, Nkrumah). Nigeria was where the Westminster type of parliamentary democracy seemed to promise the beginnings of a stable, multi-racial, and multi-confessional society.

Then, in a few feverish days, the whole Nigerian edifice collapsed. The prime minister, a British-style black gentleman and farseeing statesman, was kidnapped, tortured, mutilated, and killed. Many others were hunted down and assassinated, among them some five hundred officers of the army. Many people fled in terror to neighboring Togo and Dahomey. A military dictatorship was then set up which the western press decided for the nth time to regard as a guarantee of future peace and stability. One wonders how long it will last.

Nigeria today, after the departure of the white government with its severe but pacifying rule, seems to reproduce chapters of nineteenth century South West African history. South West Africa was originally inhabited by Bushmen, of the same primitive tribes which roamed South Africa before the whites and the Bantu arrived. Later (non-black) Hottentot tribes and black Bantu came from the east and south, parts of the migrations which had begun centuries before, originating in the region of Africa's Great Lakes. Each tribe and sub-tribe brought its special skills, attachment to chiefs, ways

of herding cattle, primitive industries, and the myths and
legends of its origin. Some were more agricultural and
peaceful, like the Ovambo, who settled in the north;
others like the Nama and the Herero, were cattle breed-
ers, nomadic, turbulent; yet others like the Damara,
proved easy to subdue, and they became Herero and
Nama slaves. In the Rehoboth Gebiet, the Basters settled.
When I first saw them, I noted their light skins, similar in
its whitish yellowness to that of the Chinese; they also
had other Mongolic features: slanted eyes and broad
faces. Then there are the Coloureds, who as in South
Africa, are a mixture of Malay, Hottentot, and sometimes
white blood, but also with black influence. Other pure
Bantu live in the Caprivi Zipfel, the Okavango, and
Kaokoveld.

Then there are the still remaining Bushmen. Of non-
black origin, their skin is a brown-tinted yellow, their eyes
slanted; they are of small, fragile stature, but extremely
resistant to hardship, trained by the tough conditions in
which they have lived for untold centuries. Not only are
they nomadic, but they never knew agriculture or cattle
breeding, built only temporary shelters, and carried their
few possessions in a bag made of the stomach of an
antelope. They kill with bow and arrow, and use, like the
people of the Kaokoveld, sharp stones to skin the animal.
Their women, who in mature, child-bearing age, look like
our ten-year-old girls, carry their beauty equipment, a
snuff-like powder, in tortoise shells, and marry the man
who "shoots" them with a small arrow specially made for
the purpose, obviously by Cupid.

Long before the white men arrived in South West Africa, the Bushmen were hunted down by the Bantu, and most cruelly killed whenever found. This is why they retreated into the desolate wastelands of the Kalahari Desert where nobody followed them. The white authorities began to protect them in the last century, punished raids against them, and managed to stop their extermination. But even today, the Bushman is scared of the black men; if a Bantu is around, a Bushman dares not address a white directly, but only through the Bantu, whom centuries' suffering taught him to recognize as his superior.

South West Africa's fascinating and cruel history is worthy of a Homer's or Shakespeare's pen. Only the Ovambo in the north were relatively peaceful and undisturbed, perhaps since they had a settled life, cultivating an unrewarding soil and keeping their herds. But to the south of them, there was permanent warfare and incredible acts of cruelty. The Nama and Herero, joined by the Damara, Baster, and other tribes, killed and burned each others' settlements and people mercilessly, with only occasional peaceful periods brought about by missionaries and lasting less time then was needed for the signatories to ride away from the range of a rifle shot. There was a kind of fatality in this mutually inflicted horror; in the intervals of their clashes with the Nama, the Herero's herds would increase out of proportion, which would force them to expand their grazing areas. This in turn would be the cause of a new attack by the Namas. When there was no warfare, the traditional pasture soon became overstocked, and grazing would deteriorate, together with the condition of the stock. The chain of tragedies was never-ending.

Throughout the entire century, the situation, even among the members of the same tribe, was so bad that at one time (in 1854) the Nama chiefs agreed that "every Nama who wanted to go into the tribal territory of another chief must get a pass from his own chief. Anyone who did not have a pass was liable to be regarded as vagrant, and was then to be treated as one."*

The white men round out the multi-faceted population picture. The nineteenth century saw scattered settlements of South African Germans, Finns, and Englishmen established. They were mostly farmers, traders, and missionaries. As elsewhere in Africa, the missions played the essential civilizing role. Their detailed history should one day be written, because it would show what the Christian combination of faith, fearlessness, and practical mind can do in reclaiming human beings from underdevelopment. Engraved forever in my memory is a Catholic mission station near Runtu in the Okavango area. Sister Leopoldina, a sixty-year-old German nun, speaking the Bantu languages with heavy Swabian accent, has created a home and school for girls, whom she saves from the gruesome parental habit of selling them into prostitution at an early age, and then into marriage. When she arrived some thirty years ago, parents argued that they got at

---

* What did such a treatment entail? Mutilation of hands and feet, tying the prisoner to a pole and beating him to death, putting him under the wheels of a heavy wagon, burning him alive, starving, skinning and quartering him, etc. No wonder that the native population decreased to a great extent.

least something, a piece of cloth or cooking utensils or cattle, for selling their daughters to rich old men. As for the boys, they were not sold but needed at home to guard the cattle. Sister Leopoldina used to plead with the parents to entrust the children to her, telling them that religion and education are better builders of happiness than early prostitution and slavery in a loathed husband's hut. Later she had to plead with the girls themselves against their habit of disappearing into the jungle to join their lovers. "My desires are as keen as yours," she used to tell them, "but I resist through prayers to the Lord." ("Never show yourself," the sister told me, "superior to these youngsters, but just as frail, human and sinful as they are. Then show them that only religion and love of the Lord enable all of us to overcome our weaknesses.")

One day early in her endeavors, Sister Leopoldina was put to a harsh test. With some children around her, she visited a not-too-distant village. On the way back in the darkening forest, the children suddenly began to shout, "The lion, the lion is coming!" and they disappeared in every direction. The young woman remained alone, resigned, but steadfast in her faith. Around her was the jungle with its thousand shapes and sounds—and roar of lions. But no lion came. Half an hour later, the children returned to her, "It was we and our families who imitated the lions," they explained. "We wanted to see if you are really not afraid of dying, if your faith in God makes you feel as you so often tell us."

The children's admiration for her was followed by that of the parents, until the day in the classroom she hit a boy who refused to learn his lesson. The boy's father was a chief. It was like spanking a prince's son, and the chief arrived the following day, surrounded by his tribesmen. "You will have to stand trial," they told her.

Sister Leopoldina went to the old priest, head of the small mission. "I could save you from the ordeal," he said to her, "by talking to the chief and persuading him to desist. But your authority before these people would be lost forever. You must let them proceed."

Solemnly the chief asked Sister Leopoldina to justify herself. "Now, chief," she addressed him, "if your mule or your ox refuses stubbornly once, twice, three times to do what you tell him to, don't you take a stick and prod him? The same way with your boy; he is in school here for his own good, but he is stubborn like a mule and won't do his work. What would you do with him?"

"Take this stick," the chief answered, "and hit the boy if he disobeys you!"

Other whites came, of course, with less constructive ambitions, although the general poverty did not attract the great powers when the "scramble for Africa" began. The Germans who settled on the coast at Swakopmund and Luderitz asked for a colonial status, and the British in South Africa hoped also to see the territory annexed. But London only proclaimed its right on Walvis Bay and the surrounding area (1878); the Germans, almost by default, turned South West Africa into a colony (1884).

German rule was harsh, but harshness was needed to put an end to the incessant warfare decimating the tribes. The last decade before World War I continued to be the record of massacres, villages burned, cattle stolen, tribes forced to flee into the desert where they perished. While the Ovambo, the largest tribe of South West Africa, were living in peace on both sides of the border with Angola, the Herero and the Nama were still locked in wars of extermination. They agreed on one thing only, to reduce the Damaras to slave status, and treat them, as well as captured Bushmen, with incredible cruelty. The Herero, already punished by their traditional enemies, the Nama, were finally crushed by German colonial forces, after a last rebellion. They did not recover until this day, when they are once more on the increase numerically. But they have always resisted cooperation with whites and blacks alike.

Not until 1907 was the state of sectional warfare in South West Africa declared to have ended. It had cost the Germans more than two thousand casualties, the Herero lost about 65,000 people, the Damara 17,000, the Nama 8,000. Since the 1915 South African occupation, no more fighting has taken place, and the peaceful conditions are reflected in the census; in 1921, the non-white population of South West Africa numbered only 190,000; now, forty years later, the figure is up to 467,000.

The first World War extended Anglo-German hostilities to South West Africa too. South African troops (South Africa had been a British-Boer union since 1910 with dominion status) marched into the territory and forced the German garrison's surrender. So, at the end of the war, South West Africa first came under South African occupation, by right of conquest. In 1920 the League of

Nations entrusted the territory to the South African government as a mandate.* It was understood that, as in all other territories under mandate, South Africa would provide for the protection of South West Africa to secure peace and orderly progress, in harmony with the interests of all sections of the population. The laws of the mandate power were applicable in South West Africa too; and an annual report was to be submitted to the mandate commission of the League of Nations, recording the phases of development. It should be noted that South West Africa constituted a "C" mandate, a unique case by which the League of Nations recognized the utterly primitive conditions of the territory, where no previous political structure prevailed. In other words, for all practical purposes, the government of South Africa obtained a free hand in regard to its rights and duties, always in the spirit of what the mandate termed the "sacred trust of civilization."

Among the many unfinished matters left by the breezy settlements of the first World War, the mandate question was perhaps the last that the contracting great powers expected one day to erupt. Only the decolonization following the second World War brought this question again to light, and left it tragically unresolved.

* * *

Article Twenty-two of the Covenant specified that South West Africa belonged to those lands which "owing to the sparseness of their population or their remoteness from the centers of civilization, or their geographic contiguity to the territory of the Mandatory . . . can best be administered under the laws of the Mandatory as integral

* See Appendix for text of mandate.

portions of its territory." It followed from this Article that the mandate authorized South Africa to apply its own laws, adapted to local circumstances, and to maintain sufficient force to uphold law and order. This was not annexation; but President Wilson of the United States did not rule out its probability when he stated, "It is left to the Union of South Africa to make [its administration] so attractive that South West Africa will come into the union of its own free will. If South Africa manages South West Africa as well as she manages her own country, then she will be married to South West Africa."

The history of South West Africa between the two World Wars remained rather eventless. The important thing was to develop it economically, so as to lay the foundations of progress. Apparently the mandate commission of the League of Nations found no fault with South African administration, although South Africa, still a British dominion, might have found it tempting to go slowly in developing a land with an uncertain future.

Since the German days, the territory had been divided into a southern "police zone" (so-called because the white men's laws were applied there) and a northern territory administered according to tribal law. It must be understood that the tribes are not as western liberal thinkers believe, anachronistic museum pieces, and their members manipulable pawns. Here, as everywhere in Africa, tribal traditions, ways of life, and practices are so well rooted in the continent's conditions that to uproot them by imposing rapid changes would be both difficult and uselessly cruel. Thus, tribal administration was left largely intact in the northern third of South West Africa, and was only assisted by white administrators who aimed to improve the general standard of living, not to destroy what was healthy and constructive.

Again it should not be forgotten that South West Africa, in spite of its vastness, is poor and underpopulated, and only a small percentage of its soil is economically tillable. Since the native tribes cannot be expected to turn into modern industrial nations, even in several generations, it was imperative that the white man, having the know-how and the capital, should be encouraged to develop the territory and associate the natives gradually with his work, achievements, and ways of looking at orderly progress in the twentieth century. Hence the encouragement given by the South African government to various firms and entrepreneurs, already existing on the territory before the mandate, and to those which moved in since then. Such enterprises include the large diamond-mining concessions along the Atlantic Coast from the Orange River mouth and well beyond Luderitz; fishing and fish canning companies in Luderitz and Walvis Bay; miners for copper, tin, lead, and other minerals at Tsumeb (a Canadian holding), at Uys (South African holding), and elsewhere. In addition there is a growing number of secondary industries, farms for karakul pelts, and scientifically cultivated farms for wheat and other produce.

A considerable difficulty for economic development is the distance of these factories, mines, and farms from each other and from their natural markets in South Africa. The terrain is such that road and railroad construction is extremely costly, and this cost must be added when export of merchandise is envisaged. Similar considerations apply to the merchandise imported, mainly from South Africa. If prices are nevertheless not higher than in the Republic, this is due to subsidies, a low tax rate, and the fact that other developments, for example, road and air communications, are partly financed by South Africa.

It is then fair to say that South West Africa has lived now for more than a generation in an economic symbiosis with the Republic. This fact encouraged Marshal Smuts, soon after the second World War, to consult the United Nations about the advisability of annexing South West Africa. The international body "took note" of South Africa's desire to turn the relationship of the two territories into a permanent link (thus implementing President Wilson's prevision of a "marriage" between them), but rejected it on the ground that the black inhabitants had not yet reached the stage of political maturity "enabling them to express themselves on such an important question."

South Africa has continued to administer the territory until this day, without however recognizing any obligation to submit annual reports to the United Nations Trusteeship Committee. The South Africans' argument is that the United Nations is not the legal successor to the League of Nations, and that South Africa did not enter into treaty obligations with the Trusteeship Committee concerning the administration of South West Africa.*

* In the terms of the South Africans' contention: "No provision was made in the United Nations charter for supervision by any UN organs in respect of mandatory administration. The United Nations created its own system of trusteeship and new agreement was required to bring any territory into the system." This is also the conclusion reached by the World Court in its Advisory Opinion of 1950.

It is from this time that we can date the complete divorce of the theses held respectively by the South African government and the United Nations. Pretoria maintains that its contractual relationship in the matter of the mandate has come to an end with the liquidation of the League of Nations. This contention is founded on fact; at the last session of the League, after the second World War (1946), the Chinese delegate suggested the transfer of competence for the territories under mandate from the mandate commission to the trusteeship committee of the United Nations. This proposal was rejected. Later South Africa submitted another solution by indicating its willingness to renegotiate the issue with the great powers that had set up the League of Nations and its various organs. But this suggestion too was rejected. The result of all this is that South Africa to this day is fulfilling its role as mandatory power with the legal status of South West Africa remaining undefined. It is, however, clear that from the point of view of international law, what has been Pretoria's accountability concerning South West Africa has lapsed.

The position of the United Nations is not so much based on law and legal precedence as on an ideological stand. This bias is shown by the UN insistence that it was under no obligation to renegotiate the status of South West Africa with Pretoria, but that it simply inherited the arrangements concluded by the League of Nations—as if the real history of mankind has begun only in 1920 with the League of Nations, which was an effort which ended in failure, to unify the world under one directing body.

But even if this attempt was followed by another one (incidentally like the first not expressing any "consensus" except the supposed common interests of the victors) this does not mean that there is here a continuity, institutional, historical, or otherwise. The view that there is such a continuity is naturally combated by South Africa, although its government decided to submit, even during the years of unresolved controversy, some reports to the United Nations as an act of courtesy. However, some South African legal experts argue that since the League no longer exists, the real status of South West Africa ought to be once more what it had been before the setting up of the mandate. In other words, that by right of conquest in 1915, South Africa has the right of annexing the territory and administering it as it did until 1920, when the validity of the mandate started.

So went the legal aspects of controversy concerning South West Africa until 1950. It is undeniable, however, that the evolution of the United Nations in the late '50s and the '60s has considerably altered the way the antagonists now look at it. This is not the place to enumerate the various advisory opinions, decisions and hearings held by, or handed down in the United Nations since 1950 by the Trusteeship Committee, the Committee on South West Africa, the Committee on Colonialism, and the General Assembly. We shall summarize these when we deal with the so-called South West Africa case before the World Court at The Hague. In anticipation, it should be mentioned nevertheless that what used to be, in the late 1940's, a constructive channel of negotiations, the General

Assembly, and other international organs of the United
Nations, has become an arena of international anarchy,
where decisions are imposed either by the powerful, or by
the demagogues.*

Just as a court is a distributor of justice on the basis of
respect for existing law, but is not an expression of a fickle
public opinion, so the United Nations ought not to have
become a docile instrument of an even less definable
"world opinion," particularly since in one decision after
another it becomes increasingly clear that certain groups,
most often the so-called Afro-Asian bloc, impose their will
on timid and opportunistic members who dare not mark
their opposition. The timid are afraid that, if rebuffed by
the West, the Afro-Asians might throw their weight (the
weight of verbosity rather than of substance!) to the
Communist side. Hence, a policy of double standards has
been quite shamelessly adopted by the United Nations, so
as to please its most radical members. How can one, under
these conditions, speak of objective attitudes with regard
to South West Africa, when one of the main objectives of
the Afro-Asian block, and of the committees filled by

* The world had to enter the shining and virtuous twentieth century
of ours to witness the international lawlessness and might-is-right behavior that has become nearly universal. The Afro-Asian nations attempt
and often succeed in excluding such nations from international bodies
whose internal policies they dislike. This has happened again and again
at ILO, the International Postal Union, International Conference on Education. Even more unexpected and deplorable is the lawlessness of the
British government. When Mr. Wilson decided to "crush Rhodesia" his
government forbade the rightly respectable Lloyd Insurance Company,
a private firm, to make payments to families of deceased persons in
Rhodesia. The lawlessness preached and practiced by London is a sad
signpost on the road to universal moral and legal degeneracy on which
we are traveling.

them and their obedient colleagues of other nations (among them some Communist ones) is to bring chaos and destruction to the territory's administrator, the South African government?

The dice are thus loaded against South Africa and its case and arguments concerning the future of South West Africa from the beginning. And yet, the charges brought by the various organs of the United Nations against the South African administration of South West Africa are of such a grave nature that every effort ought to be made to further an objective and factual discussion of the case. These charges, if true, even if partially true, would be unconcealable, and South Africa ought to be made to answer them; if on the other hand, they cannot be substantiated, then the accusers should be exposed, and South Africa vindicated.

Let me list these charges, which have been made in a rather haphazard fashion, unsystematically, and with frequent self-contradiction. Among them are charges of genocide; of robbing the natives of their land; destroying their cattle under the pretext that they suffer from hoof-and-mouth disease; the restriction of natives to menial jobs; putting obstacles in the way of their selling cattle; inadequate schooling and the maintenance of schools merely as window dressing; finally, the maintenance by South Africa of military bases in the territory (the term used is "militarization") with aggressive intent directed against the indigenous population and eventually against neighboring countries.

Here is how Mr. Moses Garoeb, of the South West

Africa People's Organization (SWAPO), summed up the charges before the special committee of the United Nations at a meeting held in New York on July 30, 1962: "The history of [his] people had been written in the blood of innocent men, women, and children, and it was a matter simply of fighting and dying for survival. They had been victims of exploitation, subjugation, and enslavement; political leaders were being deported and imprisoned daily and past laws were being strengthened and enforced more brutally. There was no justice to be expected for Africans."*

Such accusations are either true or false; they do not admit of subtly-argued gray shades. The reason why I traveled to South West Africa was to see it for myself, because in such matters it is dangerous merely to listen to hearsay or read reports. But before I give an account of what I observed there, let me mention in anticipation two events which cast a disturbing shadow on the veracity of the witnesses responsible for these charges.

Not being content with the speed with which the various UN committees proceeded against South Africa, one of the first decisions of the Organization of African Unity, founded in Addis Ababa, in May, 1960, was to request two member states, Ethiopia and Liberia, to press earlier-brought charges against South Africa concerning South West Africa before the World Court. These charges, let it be said in passing, contained nothing original; they were taken from the repertory of denunciations made at the

* Text as stated in "Report of the Special Committee for South West Africa." 17th Session, Supplement No. 12, Page 9, United Nations.

forum of the United Nations. But what should astonish all is that *no witnesses were called* to the bar at the World Court by Mr. Ernest A. Gross, American attorney for Liberia and Ethiopia, *although the charges were based exclusively on declarations by petitioners.*

When at that point the legal team of South Africa, *which did call fourteen witnesses on its side to the court case,* offered to pay the expenses involved to get the petitioners to The Hague, Mr. Gross and his clients turned down the offer. It is legitimate to ask whether they and the petitioners on whose testimony they had built their case were worried about the interrogation by the judges and the cross examination by the South African attorneys.

The second event worth mentioning is that South Africa on March 30, 1965, invited the Court or a committee of judges to visit South West Africa for an on-the-spot inspection of the veracity of the charges. Although the decision to accept or decline was left up to the Court, the South Africans suggested that, in case of acceptance, the committee might wish to include Ethiopia and Liberia, as well as any other African country, and naturally, the Republic of South Africa itself, in its itinerary. The objective of the South Africans was obvious and unconcealed: A comparison (with regard to well-being, agricultural progress, degree of scholarization for youth, etc.) between the stardard of living of South West Africa's natives and that of other African countries, including that of the accusers would confirm Pretoria's contentions and refute the charges. The Court, by eight votes to six, finally turned down the invitation (November, 1965). It remains astonishing that Mr. Gross and his clients strenuously objected from the beginning to the Court's visit as "unnecessary, costly, inconclusive."

It is not surprising that after two such jolts, two uncomfortably close calls of their bluff, the legal team of Mr. Gross suddenly, on May 19, 1965, dropped all charges—everything from genocide to inadequate schooling—and shifted their pleadings to a totally different and much more slippery ground. We shall speak of this dramatic surprise in a later chapter.*

---

* On July 18, 1966, the International Court of Justice (World Court) dismissed the complaint by Ethiopia and Liberia by an eight to seven decision, stating that Ethiopia and Liberia did not have sufficient legal interest in their claim. See Appendix for extracts from the official summary of the decision of the Court.

CHAPTER 2

JUNGLE, DESERT, TRIBES

I SPOKE ABOVE of the great variety that nature displays in this curious land. It became visible as our plane crossed the Kalahari's endless rocky land, with its sparse vegetation. Although this desert is part of Bechuanaland, it extends into the eastern section of South West Africa. Slowly, however, the landscape changed and we were flying low over a heavily overcast sky, almost at treetop level. The light Dakota seemed to be weighted down with whipping rain, and in the brownish turmoil of the Zambesi River, we could almost guess the sinister presence of crocodiles. I was delighted to see once more the African forest landscape, threatening, impenetrable, yet as virgin as the first day of Creation.

It was only hours later, and after refueling at Francistown in Bechuanaland, that we finally landed. The pilot, a man of long experience in these parts, told us that he had "lost" the small air strip, really a kind of reinforced clearing, while slipping in and out of the thick cloud banks.

Only on our return from Francistown, the clouds slowly dispersing, did we locate the landing area. Even then, he tried it first with his wheels to see if the soil was not soaked through. On the second attempt we finally landed.

Three or four more times we were to experience similarly risky landings, although by that time we had abandoned the Dakota and changed to a small six-seater Aztec plane. Heavy rainfall for even a single hour, or a passing storm could leave the clay soil so drenched that our pilot preferred to test it before coming in for good. The government is now building hard strips because these areas are accessible only by plane, and they are now often cut off from the outside world in the rainy season.

In Ondangua, center of Ovamboland, we had to risk again a venturesome landing, since a heavy rainstorm (whose movements we witnessed, fascinated, from the air) preceded us, and the hard strip was not yet completed. How great was my surprise when later in Windhoek an opposition newspaper editor showed me triumphantly a photographic proof of what he called military installations in South West Africa; the Ondangua airstrip. (The terms of the mandate forbid the militarization of South West Africa.) I told him we would have been grateful for a good landing strip, instead of the soaked terrain, but he remained unshaken, and added that the newly completed highway from Windhoek to Ovamboland was also to serve military purposes.

To us, on the contrary, it became increasingly obvious that in all of South West Africa a gigantic battle was being conducted, not against human enemies and requiring a military buildup, but against harsh, incalculable nature, and the inbred habits of the African countryside. Let me list a few instances that we could observe and study at various stations of our itinerary.

I said that the climate in South West Africa was harsh, whimsical, and generally hot and dry. As in most of tropical and sub-tropical Africa, long periods of drought alternate with excessive downpours. Unless enormous care is taken in the cultivation of land, only the hardiest plants can survive, since everything living is battered by a relentless sun and a deluge of water. Regular water supplies exist only on the borders of the territory, the Cunene River, the Zambesi, the Okavango on the north, the Orange in the south. To harness these waters would cost enormous sums that the budget would find prohibitive; we should bear in mind that the population is less than 600,000, a figure which keeps the total revenue within modest limits. Moreover, these rivers, the Cunene, for example, form a border with other countries. To tap the energies of the Cunene, agreement had to be concluded with the Portuguese in Angola, in terms of which a hydroelectric plant would supply power to parts of South West Africa, and an irrigation system now supplies water to Ovambo farms.

In times before the white man's arrival, drought meant deprivation for thousands. This test came almost with the regularity of seasons, and those who failed to move in time, and resume a nomadic existence, were inevitably stricken by the effect of the drought: They and their cattle died. Nor was resumption of wandering an easy solution, since that meant entering lands belonging to other tribes, who refused to yield their waterholes and grazing areas. Hence, interminable conflicts. Natives did bore waterholes but in the entire northern part, an undrinkable salty water is rather close to the surface, putting a quick limit to the available supply.

With our small plane we overflew the new irrigation system in company of its planner and constructor, Dr. Wipplinger. This system, combined with newly built and durable dams, will be able to supply farms in practically all of Ovamboland. Its planners are so optimistic that they have already built an entirely new town, Oshakati, an unheard-of phenomenon among the entire population. Here neat family homes, markets, shops, restaurants, and relaxation centers are available, an entirely new way of life to which the Ovambos are expected to get accustomed gradually. Oshakati will be the center for receiving and storing the farmers' grain and other produce, and its importance is expected to be such that the government has now completed a 3.5-million-dollar hospital, entirely for the natives, with 600 beds and outpatient facilities.

Speaking of hospitals, it is interesting to note that all over Africa thousands of doctors and nurses (mostly mission sisters) tend to the needs of the population, yet for decades only Dr. Schweitzer's little hospital in Lambarene (Gabon) acquired fame and reputation. The reasons for focusing the world's attention are somewhat involved, but simply stated, I believe it was Dr. Schweitzer's fame as a liberal intellectual and theologian that endeared him to the liberal press. The latter's big disappointment came when the good doctor announced in 1961 his support for Moise Tshombe, then president of Katanga and for a few years arch-foe of the liberals during his defiance of the United Nations. From that time on there was embarrassed silence in the press about Dr. Schweitzer, and relatively few and cool comments accompanied him to his grave in 1965. Strangely, only after he had declared himself for Tshombe (and implicitly against the greatest liberal fetish, the United Nations) was Dr. Schweitzer's hospital finally described in the press factually: As a good appraiser of black mentality and family structure, Schweitzer discarded the chrome-plated equipment and fancy drugs sent to him by admirers all over the world, operated in rustic surroundings, and allowed entire families with their goats and poultry to live with the patients in little, not very hygienic, huts—something that non-liberals knew all along.

Only because it is now fashionable to disparage Dr. Schweitzer's accomplishments did Mr. Mennen Williams, consistent denigrator of the white men in Africa, admit that there are on that continent "hundreds" of white doctors who perform a better job and without world fanfare. The hospital in Oshakati is one proof of this: Its charming whitewashed rooms, its superbly equipped kitchen, the operation rooms, the dispensary make it probably the best hospital in the Southern hemisphere. Outside, a circular structure is provided for the families, who often stay on until the patient is discharged. Even cooking equipment is provided for them. Dr. Opitz, the chief physician, explained that such is the family attachment that it is often difficult to examine a new patient: Doting relatives want to keep an anxious hand on him so that the doctor has to beg them to let him do his job. In another hospital at Katima Molilo in the Caprivi jungle, teams of two doctors from South Africa spend a month each giving medical aid, performing operations, and prescribing the necessary drugs. The chief obstacle to their work is the extremely strong hold that the witch doctor has on the natives. They first consult him and submit with traditional docility to his magic. Only when their case gets worse, but even then only after securing the witch doctor's permission, do they finally come to the hospital. Often it is too late.

Oshakati, with its promise of great progress, was now behind us. The Ovambos whom we had met, the secretary of the tribal council, the inspector of education, the storekeeper where I bought a good pair of shoes for the bush, are the emerging leaders of the tribe, the largest and most forward-looking of the territory. I admired their realism in envisaging the future. About a year ago, thirty officials, chiefs, headmen, etc., were invited to visit the Transkei, the first Bantustan set up as a logical consequence of apartheid policies. On their return, and in conversation with me, the visitors admitted that the Xhosa nation is considerably ahead of them, whose association with South Africa dates only from 1920. "We need more educated men," both the inspector of schools and the tribal secretary told me. "And we must step up the education of girls," an issue which is the true point of resistance of the average African to progress.

If the Ovambos are still behind the Xhosas, the Bush-men are undoubtedly the most primitive people one meets in Africa, possibly in the world. Our encounter with the Stone Age world took place in Tsumkwe, where Bantu Affairs commissioner McIntyre and his wife have been struggling for years to lift the Bushmen out of their increasing misery. This was one of the many occasions when I had to remind myself how completely ignorant the outside world is with its cliches, smugly categorical state-ments and holier-than-thou attitude. I had also to admit to myself the utter immorality of the suggestions and solu-tions that comfortable intellectuals in western capitals wish to impose on an incredibly complex situation. I think the case of the Bushmen might serve as an object lesson for those still redeemable from the abstraction-ridden atmosphere of western council chambers.

I read in the earlier-quoted "Special Committee Report of the United Nations" the following sentence: According to the petitioners (South West Africans giving testimony at the United Nations), "Bushmen were being hired sup-posedly as servants, but were treated like prisoners, being left barefooted and naked, without shelter and exposed to the summer heat, the winter cold and rain, and they were receiving no pay." This is in Paragraph 50 (there are 57 of them) enumerating all the things the white men com-mitted against non-whites. If the other 56 points are as truthful as the one just quoted, we can finally understand why the same witnesses were not called to testify at the World Court in The Hague.

Let us now look at the facts. The Bushmen, forced to

flee in the seventeenth and eighteenth century before the advancing white and black men, began to settle in the Kalahari Desert. "Settle" is not the right word because they have always been nomadic up to this very day, eating smaller animals, even moles and rats, never building permanent shelters, never wearing more than a loin cloth. Their treatment at the hands of the Bantu was nothing short of horrible; the latter literally hunted them down, inflicted gruesome punishment after enslaving them, but most often killing them outright, not with gun or knife, but with sticks and stones.

Looking into their leathery, withered faces, at their brownish yellow color and their eyes full of resignation before an incredibly tough existence, one feels a mixture of pity, incomprehension, and embarrassed strangeness. One would like to extend a helping hand to facilitate their crossing over the abyss of prehistory, but how to go about it? Mr. McIntyre has no such hesitation. The Bushman, he tells us, has reached the end of his nomadic existence. The white man's laws protect their survival, but whites and blacks move in on them, cultivate the land, open mines, build airports and cities. The territory on which they have been roving keeps getting smaller; progress destroys their way of life, and not even their resilience to climate and scarcity is of any avail.

The only solution, as McIntyre and the government see it, is to settle them, teach them to raise cattle, cultivate the land, build huts, and learn a trade. All this is urgent, yet it must be done slowly, because one does not transplant a savage creature from hard nature into modern

comfort in a few years, even decades. We saw the workshop where McIntyre teaches them how to work copper
into bracelets, match boxes, tiny arrows and other items.
He intends to sell the objects on commission to Capetown
and Durban tourist shops so as to accustom the Bushmen
to the concept of money, earning, saving. "It is essential,"
he tells us, "that we should not turn their hard life too
suddenly into a kind of affluence. Rather the hardship of
making a living should be impressed upon them in their
new environment also."

These are wise words, and not only words. As we
wanted to take a picture of Mrs. McIntyre tending the
sick under an enormous baobab tree, the commissioner
told us brusquely: "I cannot allow it. These are human
beings, not strange animals or tourist attractions."

His was not the modern liberals' phony admiration for
the twentieth century "noble savage." It is part of the
necessity of dealing with concrete situations, not with
their mental reflection. McIntyre has no special admiration for the Bushmen and he severely judges them as one
man may judge others. It appears that they do not have
even the rudiments of a political structure and authority,
children do not obey their parents, couples quarrel constantly, everyone is out for himself alone, and oldsters are
abandoned near some big rock to slow starvation. This is
struggle for existence as our ancestors knew it. To "de-
frost" their primitiveness is the main task. Like Sister
Leopoldina, Mr. McIntyre, too, believes that rather than
brand-new clinics and schools, they need to be taught the
ways and means of self-help. But the government dictates

its own rhythm, which is considerably faster. Pretoria has now devised the grotesque plan of surrounding Mr. McIntyre with a team of six: an anthropologist, sociologist, a physician, an agronomist, etc. May they not distract him in his valuable task!*

Grootfontein is the main center for manpower recruitment in the Ovambo area. The administrators of the territory must solve two problems in the course of exploiting and developing it economically. On the one hand, and according to the stipulations of the mandate, South Africa is authorized to apply its own laws in South West Africa, which are grouped in this instance under the term "apartheid." The motives for applying this policy, whose merits or demerits are not the central issue of this book,** are the same in South Africa as in South West Africa: to insure the frictionless coexistence of the many ethnic communities until such time when each of them has matured sufficiently to assume the burdens and responsibilities of independence. In South West Africa there are some ten tribal groups, and Pretoria is determined to bring them separately to a workable phase of nationhood.

On the other hand, South West Africa cannot collectively advance unless its economy has before it a wide scope and less limited possibilities, both in the southern white area (the Police Zone) and the northern but also scattered native areas. At Grootfontein then arrive two

---

* If the reader now returns to the special committee statement about the mistreatment of the Bushmen, he will realize the absurd character of the statements made therein.

** I dealt with the problem of "apartheid" in my earlier book, *Africa, a Political Travelogue*, Chapter 7.

kinds of requests: from white employers, offers of employment, listing the nature of work; and acceptance of work by Ovambos to whom the conditions of work are explained. Once a contract is signed, the employer provides transportation (usually by bus to and from Grootfontein, by air to the place of work) and supply of food, lodging, medical and other services during employment period.

Whether the employment is in mines, fisheries, canning, farms, hotels, restaurants or anywhere else, the duration cannot go beyond one year, or in the case of unmarried men eighteen months. The contract is renewable, on old or new terms, indefinitely; the law requires that in between terms of work the employed person should be transported back to his native area.

One can grasp the controversial nature of this law, which deprives the worker of continous income and the employer of continuous service by a man trained to do the job. In addition, there is the necessity of retraining the worker after an interval of at least three or possibly six months and more.

Why then does Pretoria insist on maintaining this law? "Apartheid," which may be called a policy of gradual decolonization, is based on the need in this multi-national, multi-racial land to establish homelands for each race. If on the contrary, Ovambos, Namas, Bushmen, etc. became uprooted by settling together with their families near the industrial urban centers of the white territory, then integration in the long run would be inevitable. And integration, it is argued by Pretoria, means in our democratic, egalitarian age, universal suffrage, that is, in South West

Africa, the political dominance of Ovambos (45% of the total population) over the rest. The situation would lead back directly to the nineteenth century, where one tribe attempted to rule over others.

It would certainly be a step heavy with consequences if the Ovambo were encouraged to leave Ovamboland permanently. For the American reader, accustomed to pull up his roots and move thousands of miles across the continent, this problem does not seem to be a problem at all. But let us look briefly at what would follow if South West Africa also adopted such a mobility. The Ovambo are an agricultural people, deeply attached to their land and to their tribal way of life. Leaving their land and moving to the Police Zone, they would also give up their social structure, legal system, veneration for ancestors. As a Canadian couple's Ovambo servant told them when they offered to move him and his family permanently to the white area, he does not desire to give up his farm back home and does not wish to expose his children to the "bad ways" of town life. He preferred to interrupt his service every year and return for a few months to live with his family on their farm.

This situation, which is at the core of "apartheid" must necessarily have many critics, among them bitter ones. But it must be admitted that most of the attacks against the system spring from emotionalism, and worse, from misplaced ideological preoccupations. After having visited a good many places of employment where this system is applied, I should like to take stock of the pros and cons, and speak of eventual reasonable improvements.

There are two primary considerations in the matter: one that South West Africa should be developed to the full measure of its economic and manpower resources. The other is that in view of Africa's more than uncertain future, even if a certain unbalance exists in the treatment of various population groups, this is not an unreasonable price to pay for present stability and prosperity as well as growth into future autonomy. In other words, while apartheid imposes and meticulously regulates differentiation according to race, one look at events in the rest of Africa will convince us that, at the present time at least, there is no alternative; or rather, that the alternative is chaos, destruction, misery, and mutual extermination by tribes, parties, political and military cliques.

Having said this, let us now look at the situation of Ovambo workers and the consequences deriving from their situation. The first observation is that there is a wide variety of jobs accommodating the various skills and also wide variety of conditions according to the management's employment policy, needs, ability to pay, and offer of fringe benefits. The second observation is that almost all of them acquire skills which they can then put to good use in their own land, either temporarily between contracts, or permanently if they save enough money so as not to have to return to work in the Police Zone, but start some business of their own at home. In other words, not only money is coming constantly into Ovamboland, but the farmer or shepherd who had left returns as carpenter; truck, tractor, or bulldozer driver; mechanic; mason; medical assistant; male nurse; shopkeeper; construction worker; or entrepreneur. Part of the work now done in the Ovamboland irrigation project uses the skilled workers now available in the area; many of the general stores now open started with capital earned in the form of wages in the Police Zone; the furniture factory at Oshakati employs carpenters who learned their trade at Walvis Bay or Oranjemund or Tsumeb.

Trades and skills acquired in this fashion are not superficial things. It is, therefore, not true that the system prevailing in South West Africa retards the natives. There are today far more skilled workers among them in South Africa and South West Africa than in the northern two-thirds of Africa, in the independent countries.

I visited, for example, the aptitude test center selecting workers for the Tsumeb mines for all sorts of tasks, among them very complicated ones. Mechanical skill, intelligence, even leadership qualities are tested according to procedures used in white areas (in the Johannesburg industrial region) and in the western world. The tested workers are then employed at jobs according to their aptitudes; nothing prevents them from putting these skills to good use on their return to their territories. This is an important point because critics denounce the homelands as a convenient and cheap labor reserve for white entrepreneurs and the recruitment system as a form of slave market. But the thesis stands or falls depending on the government's determination to develop the homelands agriculturally, commercially, and industrially. There can be no doubt entertained that indeed such is the government's intention. Nor do the natives constitute a cheap labor force. It is true that the wages start at the low level and only in exceptional instances do they become considerable. But the workers earn much more than just their wages, and every company discovers new ways of extending benefits to its workers, beginning with payment in almost every case higher than what the law prescribes as a minimum.*

The native worker pays no taxes except a nominal one to his chief upon returning to his land. This is according to tribal custom. On the other hand he receives benefits of all kinds. It is a universal practice all over southern Africa and gratefully welcomed by all in Mozambique as well as in South West Africa that workers receive only part of their wages at work, the rest is transferred by the employing company to the worker's family back home. In this way one legend entertained by those who remember the company towns in Europe and the United States is invalidated as far as South West Africa is concerned; the company does not attempt to take away with one hand the amount it disburses with the other. The bulk of the worker's earning arrives to his family thus increasing the latter's purchasing power, as well as the total income of the native area. And of course, these totals amount to millions of dollars. At the Oranjemund diamond mines the

---

* Wage raises have resulted lately in an unexpected phenomenon. Earning now in eight or nine months what they used to earn in one year, many workers decide to quit before the expiration of their term of contract. Yet the desire of earning more is likely to catch up with them as it has with their Bantu brothers in the Republic. In the latter, Bantu earnings have increased steadily over the past years. In the past two years there has been a 44% increase in the total Bantu income, representing between 20% and 23% of the net national income of all races.

workers may open a savings account with an interest of six percent per annum, payable together with the capital to the family. Let us note that the interest rate in South Africa is about half of this, and that the unusually high rate at Oranjemund is due to the company's intention to encourage saving among its black employees.

This does not mean that during a contract period the worker cannot afford certain comforts and luxuries for his own consumption and also purchases in view of sending them home and collecting until the day of his departure. When he finally gets off the bus in the village or kraal, he is loaded with presents like a St. Nicholas. His buying habits are becoming smarter every year. I talked with the general store manager at Oranjemund who has most interesting things to tell about his customers. The latter not only know exactly what they want, but their preference goes to certain patterns, for example, in textiles, and when they like one they buy an entire roll, sending it home to their women folk. This explains why we saw in Ovamboland groups of women wearing dresses and handkerchiefs made of the same material, of bright colors, large flowers, or other designs. In many instances, the workers buy their own sewing machines (at Oranjemund the company supplies them) and make themselves the dresses they then mail to wives and mothers.

Even so, the wages would appear low in view of the growing purchasing appetite and opening opportunities to spend, if the collective benefits and facilities were not increasing at the same time. Medical care, schooling, veterinarian service for cattle are entirely free, as are also the irrigation costs, all sorts of aids to farming, and training or re-training in mechanical and industrial skills. As mentioned before, during the twelve-month period of work, all basic needs are covered including overalls and other work clothes. One sees frequently in Ovamboland farmers with brand new overalls with the initials C.D.M. (Consolidated Diamond Mines) marked on the back: the last and best-kept piece they took along on leaving the mines.

It would be an exaggeration to say that the various companies like the system of interrupted terms of work periods. They find it rather costly to have to retrain many, especially skilled workers who may forget during time spent home in the kraal how to drive an expensive bulldozer or how to lubricate parts of a machine. The management, however, understands the overall benefits of an apartheid policy and of the periodic contract system, which is its corollary. Yet, almost every one of them applies at times to the competent ministry for permission to keep certain key personnel on a permanent basis which means that the latter's families also move away from the homeland and join the head of the family. Whether the number of these "de-tribalized" natives will increase in the future, as more industries move in and more towns are established is anybody's guess.

One must, however, stress again the positive aspects of the system, or at least its basis in incontrovertible reality. The Ovambo, as an African, is still generally a farmer attached to the land much more than the European used to be before the industrial revolution. In Ovamboland even the school inspector is a farmer, since the land represents not only security but the link with the tribe and also contact with the ancestors. A similar attachment exists between the farmer and his cattle; it took years to persuade the Ovambo (or, for example, the Masai in Kenya) to part with his oxen for purposes of selling them to meat packing plants or slaughter houses. The Ovambo though less than the Hindu considers his cattle as somehow members of his kraal, as a being with a soul or at least spirits. Even today he might be unwilling to sell cattle outside the homeland, although he takes them now to local markets and abattoirs. At times of disease among the cattle it is similarly difficult to persuade the owner to have them quarantined or, if necessary, shot in order to protect the healthy beasts of the herd.*

The drawback of the contract system as it is practiced is that the worker, upon returning to his kraal, falls back into old habits: he takes it easy, sits all day in front of the hut, drinking and smoking, and lets the women work as they have done from times immemorial. Or he may spend his hard-earned money on the purchase of a used car, purely as a status symbol, and when it breaks with ill use,

---

* Like any peasant, the Ovambo too is heartbroken when this happens although they submit to the veterinarian's verdict. One can be sure that, contrary to the mendacious allegations of witnesses, given so malevolent and naive credit by the United Nations Special Committee, no cattle are destroyed by the "white authorities" except for good medical reasons. Yet I know of cases when western journalists, out of malice, and driven by the desire to incite their readers, took pictures in South West Africa, showing "natives behind barbed wire." In reality, these were pictures of fenced-in areas for diseased cattle, sadly contemplated by their owners from the outside. This is typical of the nature of almost all reports by foreign journalists about South Africa and South West Africa.

he lets it stand and rust by the kraal fence. How many times did I see the chassis of a car beyond repair stand incongruously in the puddle outside, representing the only "western" commodity as far as the horizon! Is this the fault of the "system," or more particularly, of apartheid? Even if we did not observe the same phenomena in independent African countries, we still would have to conclude that these are results of several interlocking habits, innate conservatism, tribal cohesion, and local mentality. Had I not known it from innumerable previous observations, the stories Sister Leopoldina told us at Runtu would have pointed at the heart of the difficulty of social transformation. The black woman is still largely inaccessible to education. The tribal secretary in Ondangua told me, among the first things as we sat down in his office for a long and instructive conversation: A girl may start going to school, then at fourteen she suddenly gets married or is sold into marriage. Her education, hardly begun, is interrupted, and from then on she becomes a combination of child-bearer and workhorse. The missions (in this area Finnish and Catholic) make heroic efforts to educate women, the centers of the family and the deepest influence on children; but they can only skim the surface and do not succeed in altering the imprint of habit which remains the dominant force all over the African continent.

CHAPTER 3

THE WHITE LADY

THE FLIGHT over the Etosha Pan is unforgetable. We truly felt lifted from ordinary impressions and dimensions, perhaps because of a rare combination of circumstances. When our small Aztec plane left Tsumeb, heavy dark clouds were already gathering and it seemed risky to defy them, since the forecast predicted storms in the whole area. After fifteen minutes in the air the quality of the surrounding light began to change; it became distinctly other-worldly as it filtered through the barrage of clouds.

Suddenly in the distance there appeared the white patch of the Namutoni Fort built more than a half a century ago by the Germans, a typical, European, fortress castle with crenalated towers, and now used as a tourist camp. Beyond Namutoni which we circled for more weather reports, clear land became visible like the silvery thread of a sea in the distance. It was the Etosha Pan, an enormous stretch of gray flat surface, with nothing on it except the sparsest of vegetation, and patches of water with herds of animals drinking at them.

I have flown above many deserts and was later to observe, from above the Namib, a thousand-mile-long coastal strip of golden sand dunes. But while a sandy desert lives because of the constant change of forms that the winds chase, the contour of the bottom of the Etosha Pan remains unaltered like a moonscape; up in our little plane, we felt as if we were riding over an ocean suspended between two flat surfaces.

The sky was first to change and we saw terrible storms raging in the not far distance, forming mushroom-shaped clouds. The curtain of rain seemed to be the stem, and above it, darkly flowered, the celestial water reservoir. Below, buffaloes, ostriches, antelopes, zebras were peacefully drinking and raising their frightened heads as we passed them, and multi-chromatic birds fluttered out of our way. But three days later, crossing the other end of the Etosha Pan, we could not have told that it was the same world: a sea covered everything as far as one saw; the rain had come.

The fascinating thing about the desert world is that it is more alive with vegetation and animals than any luxuriant public park in our cities. Such a park is essentially dead because controlled, watched, kept to artificial dimensions. But the desert is constantly changing. What you see in daytime as dry and desolate country, miles from the coast, becomes soaked with sea water which emerges with the tide. And then, or after a passing rain storm, myriad plants show their heads, as if waking from a dormant phase. Animals, of course, know this habit of the desert, and show up at the feast that life in its inexhaustible resources has prepared for them.

An extreme case is the plant called Welwitschia, found in the desert in southern Angola and the north of South West Africa. It is like an octopus or a giant spider, four to six feet in diameter, with its lifelessly extended gray leaves. From afar you would take it for a strange rock or a bunch of dying leaves. In fact, it can become green in minutes; it stores water and other succulent juices ready for animals and Bushmen, and lives for thousands of years (it is said to be a prehistoric plant) on its roots growing many feet deep into the soil.

Compared with the fantastic world of the Etosha Pan, the village of Oshikango, right on the Angolan border, is a reassuring little paradise. In the blue sky, fat white clouds chase each other or remain suspended and assume playful shapes. Down below, the earth seems satisfied with recent rainfall, fat black or brown oxen graze and drink interminably. Children are guarding them, but they take to play as often as not, since the beasts are peaceful and hardly move. Men, many in C.D.M.-lettered overalls, are busy putting better roofs on the nearby buildings; others chat on the steps of the general store.

We walk into the home of Commissioner Burmeister. One day when South Africa ceases to be the easy target of the world's pack of ideological wolves, the story of these Bantu affairs commissioners will have to be told and

written. It will be an epic story, yet a modest one because
the performers of genuine accomplishments are usually
modest. Today, of course, in the world-wide leftist and
liberal press, these men insofar as they are known to exist
at all are described as merciless executors of an inhuman
policy. Let me, in contrast, pay tribute to them as men of
extraordinary devotion to their difficult task. Whether
they attempt to lift the Bushmen out of the Neolithic, or
tend hundreds of cases of disease, or teach primitive
natives the art of rational cultivation far above the in-
grained habits of the subsistence farming, these men are
at their work for decades, with constantly postponed
vacations (because they are indispensable), away from
civilized facilities.

Are they paternalistic with the native tribes whose well-
being and peace are entrusted to them? Of course they
are, in the same way as every man with responsibilities in
Africa is paternalistic with the blacks whether he's called
Haile Selassie, Kenyatta, Verwoerd, or Senghor. Yet they
are also the opposite of a paternalistic administrator,
because as South Africans they fervently believe in the
necessity of teaching self-help. Their thinking can be
summed up as follows: "The African has always been
provided with the minimum required for survival. Food in
one form or another is rather abundant, even though, if no
effort is made, it yields what we call an unbalanced diet.
Moreover, the kraal and tribal solidarity guarantee at
least the basic food and shelter for all members. But
beyond this level, there is an almost invincible indolence,

passivity, lack of initiative, and organizational ability. We Europeans possess these qualities because the land we originally came from was a harsh master and we had to think ahead, plan the future, provide for lean days. We had developed the concept of an incalculable future, and we prepare to meet its demands. If anything, our civilization is too future-oriented. In contrast, the black man lives in the present; if he has enough now, he does not see why he should exert himself in view of tomorrow. But the black man too will find, as western ideas penetrate irresistibly among them, that they must adjust to a new rhythm of life and work. While they resist it they also welcome it; proof is their new and real enthusiasm for getting an education, although still rather in the verbal professions such as teaching, preaching, and law rather than in engineering, chemistry, medicine, agricultural expertise, or mechanical skills. Our task and our overall policy is to show them the ways and means of doing things for themselves, to give them all the initial help, correct their early efforts, even to stand by for a long period. But they must not be led to expect that we will always do things for them, that we will remain forever responsible, that we are a kind of deities, absorbing the shock of failure and dispensing the new bounty. They must learn to fend for themselves."

I think I reproduced rather faithfully the characteristic train of thought of the Bantu affairs commissioners whom I got to know. It must be added that this is no mere abstract reasoning, and has certainly nothing to do with the chimerical and ultimately harmful do-goodism that western and not-so-western liberals practice.*

As one Bantu affairs commissioner told me, here in South West Africa, as in South Africa, there is a considerable percentage of urbanized Africans, more advanced than their rustic cousins. It would be dangerous and reprehensible to allow the difference to grow. The goal is to catch up with the urbanized Ovambo (to speak of them now) so that there should be an equality of development between the homelands and those members of their people who live in the Police Zone. (It is evident that the contract system of alternating periods serves the same purpose, namely securing the circulation of skills and permanence of contact.)

While talking with Mr. Burmeister and eating a hearty meal with his young wife and children, I thought of the vicious statements cloaked in the terminology apparently respectful of the highest ideals that I had read in the United Nations Special Committee report. There, on Page 7, it is written among other things that the African population is "deprived of all basic human rights and fundamental freedoms." This is the kind of statement calculated

---

* Mr. McIntyre, the thousand-handed commissioner of the Bushmen, told me of American sociologists who had suggested that, in order to make the Bushmen feel important, he should formally ask them for permission to remain on their land! Oh, how much ignorance and irresponsibility in one sentence! The Bushmen are nomadic, they have no land of their own; they have no tribal structure, hence no chiefs or headmen who could issue the "authorization." Among themselves they pull in every direction. "But," remarked my host, laughing, "suppose I request their permission to remain here and save this remnant from sure extinction; should I then get out when they change their minds?"

to help demagogic speakers in the General Assembly shock the ladies between coffee and cookies in clubs, and to send waves of indignation through naive students and no less naive but less excusable professors.

My visit to Mr. Burmeister was part of my investigation of the degree of autonomy of the tribal authorities. I had spoken that morning with the secretary of a tribal council, who showed me his files with all the names of the tribesmen, the receipts for taxes paid, and the budget. Then I walked over to the bank office to see what amounts had been paid out to families whose male members were transferring part of their wages from Tsumeb, Windhoek, Oranjemund, or Walvis Bay.

I could ascertain that the entire administration of tribal life was in tribal hands, including the granting to new applicants, with money saved, the right to open trading posts. I noted with surprise in their record that one recent application had been rejected. At my request, they showed me the rest of the document where it was stated that the applicant's financial backer was an outside white man; the latter's funds would have made the façading black man too strong a competition for the other traders of the area.

All civil and administrative cases are handled by the council of chiefs and headmen. Criminal cases, however, are reviewed by the commissioner for the reason illustrated by a recent contention. In a quarrel, an Ovambo lost his left hand, cut off with the blow of an ax. The mutilator was condemned to pay his victim a compensation of six heads of cattle. Yet, the mutilated man insisted that the left hand of his aggressor be cut off, too, according to the old tribal law of almost universal validity expressed also in the Old Testament: A hand for a hand, a tooth for a tooth. It took hours until the accuser was persuaded to desist, and only after the commissioner made it clear that he would never allow justice to take this form.

The following extract from tribal court deliberations will give an idea of the give-and-take of the tribal heads in whose hands rest the decision, and the commissioner who sits with them in an advisory capacity and acts as a registrar.

EXCERPTS FROM MINUTES MEETING OF THE KUKUANYAMA COUNCIL OF HEADMEN, HELD IN OHANGUENA ON THE 9TH OF FEBRUARY, 1965, DISTRICT OSHIKANGO, OVAMBOLAND, SOUTH WEST AFRICA. SUBJECT OF DISCUSSION: JUDICIAL SYSTEM OF THE UKUANYAMA TRIBE. TRIBAL COURT OHANGUENA.

BANTU AFFAIRS COMMISSIONER: I am of the opinion that too many headmen and sub-headmen take part in the proceedings of the tribal court. The court should be limited to, say, sixteen members, two from each oshilongo [subdistrict].

HEADMAN NEHAMIA: It is our custom to have many sub-headmen to try cases but there is not a fixed number.

HEADMAN ELIA: Many more than sixteen try cases.

BANTU AFFAIRS COMMISSIONER: My idea is to restrict the size of the court.

ACTING HEADMAN VOLUMBOLA (representing Headman Mengela): No, you cannot do that. There must be thirty or forty, or if we think it necessary, more to serve in the court. That is our custom and that is what the people want.

BANTU AFFAIRS COMMISSIONER: If a minimum of sixteen is laid down, perhaps provision could be made for the appointment of more subheadmen, if the headmen wish to do so. If the weather is bad, and only sixteen or twenty subheadmen turn up, they will carry on with cases.

HEADMAN ELIA: There must be a minimum of thirty-two subheadmen or representatives of the headmen, four from each oshilongo.

Other headmen signify agreement with Headman Elia.

BANTU AFFAIRS COMMISSIONER: I'll advise the Chief Bantu Affairs Commissioner. Headman Elia speaks of representatives of the headmen: Is it not only subheadmen who try cases?

ACTING HEADMAN GABRIEL (representing Headman Katamba): Certainly not. In my area many of the owners of komikunda are old men that are feebleminded, and I appoint other men of standing to help me with cases.

BANTU AFFAIRS COMMISSIONER: In other words, there are some owners of komikunda with judicial authority and others with no judicial authority.

HEADMAN NEHEMIAH: Yes. Even when trying cases, there are some headmen with authority of various ranks. We headmen, or even the subheadmen themselves, appoint leaders who have the power to give judgment whereas the other members of the court are only allowed to ask questions and give advice. They may express opinions.*

Ovamboland is a completely flat agricultural area. It is said that there is not one rock or stone in the entire country. Structures or roads which need stones must be supplied from outside, which is now made easier by the road built from Windhoek. (This is the road that news-

---

* There was further discussion on procedures followed in the individual district courts, of which there are eight in the Ukuanyama tribal area. Measures to bring about more uniformity under consideration.

paper publisher Engelbrecht told me briefly was part of the "military installations" put in place by an obviously aggressive Verwoerd government.)

The region over which we were flying on leaving the western edge of the Etosha Pan became now increasingly hilly and mountainous. Huge rocky formations rose in front of our fragile plane. When we landed at Uys mines, nothing reminded us any longer of the jungle at the Caprivi Zipfel, or the rich soil and grazing cattle around Ondangwa.

Perhaps every part of the world has some unique monument, God- or man-made, in which it glories, which becomes its emblem and symbol. In the South West history has left scarce souvenirs; two of them stand out: The cross that Bartholomeu Dias, the Portuguese discoverer, who seems to have been ubiquitous, planted near Luderitz (only a nineteenth century replica stands now), and the White Lady, a cave painting by ancient Bushmen, probably, halfway up the Brandberg, near Uys. It is debatable whether the artistic qualities of the White Lady and the surrounding brownish human and animal figures deserved an excursion, although no less a personage than the Abbé Breuil, the great French archeologist, had traveled, in 1947, all the way from Paris to study them. But I felt that our trip to South West Africa would somehow remain incomplete without this visit, amounting to a gesture of respect. If we were to see the strangely beautiful land in its length and breadth, we should also explore its dimensions in time.

The sun was beating down with all its might on this day

of January 26, mid-summer in the Southern Hemisphere, and the reddish-gray rocks reverberated its heat tenfold. We started our ascent, jumping from one rock to another, trying to avoid poisonous snakes and equally poisonous lizards which rushed in and out of crevices. We were proud to reach our destination, a cave with an overhang, in less than an hour, thoroughly soaked and panting. We found the White Lady showing not much more of herself than on previously seen photographs, but it was strange indeed that there was here a white figure, distinguishable among dark ones. There are all sorts of theories about the artists' identity. They may have been Bushmen driven up these inhospitable heights by their flatland enemies. But how did the White Lady happen to come among them? Was she a shipwreck damsel from the not very distant Skeleton Coast? An early missionary? A deity? Nobody really knows, particularly since Bushmen are not known to have painted on the walls of caves or on rocks. Perhaps the painters of these figures were not Bushmen at all, but people related, so one theory goes, to those who left similar filiform drawings in caves recently found in the Sahara.

The descent was considerably more painful. For some strange reason we almost ran, enjoying our new skill of rock-leaping. But by now the heat was pumping the resistance out of us, and under the inexorable midday sun, we conjured up images of thirsty caravans wending through the grueling desert. What a sharp pleasure an hour later to shower with cool water!

The same afternoon, after we chased antelopes, ostriches, and fox in the desert in a Land Rover, our little plane lifted us out of this picturesque valley, and we were soon flying over the Namib Desert. This is the land of the Big Nothing, at least from above, because later in the Windhoek Museum of Natural History we saw all kinds of animal specimens which live in the sand, and nourish themselves somehow. From the plane, the Namib looks like any part of sandy, rocky Arabia, with the latter's *wadis*, dried out river beds, which in the rainy season carry shallow but rapid waters. Camels are there, too, descendants of the animals imported for police patrol. Now the police use Land Rovers, and the camels roam undisturbed in ever larger herds.

It is an exhilarating experience to discover the ocean. No student remains unmoved by the "anabasis" of the ten thousand Greeks, who, diminished in number, but undaunted, ran down the mountains shouting Tlalassa! at the sight of the Black Sea. For a week we had flown and driven through varied lands, and were now flying in the direction of the Atlantic Ocean; its icy waves were battering the sand dunes, and the low-lying fog which covered it at nightfall was creeping over the land, making for an unsure landing.

Our meeting with the ocean recalled in less dramatic colors the story of a group of Boer trekkers, a curious chapter of South West Africa's nineteenth century annals. On the ground of political dissatisfaction, but even more strongly impelled by a mystical Calvinist restlessness, several hundreds of Boers pulled up from Transvaal in the 1870's, and took once more to the jungle. With the Bible to give them spiritual strength, they crossed in their covered wagons the entire breadth of Bechuanaland and South West Africa. The trek lasted for years, and its members endured adventures, attacks, and hardships. They themselves did not know what kept them going, but they continued in northwesterly direction. At one point, south of Ovamboland, they decided to dispatch a group of some twenty horsemen to explore what lay ahead, while the others settled down to rest. The horsemen rode for weeks, until one afternoon, going through the Namib, they became attentive to a steady murmur. None of them had ever seen the ocean, and they were anxiously guessing. Was it the noise of approaching horses; of a distant storm; of earthquake? Finally, they galloped up the high sand dunes, and saw the bright surface of the water. The story goes on of course, and it is by no means less adventurous than the first part. A Coloured merchant took them into his affection and he began negotiating the purchase of the Reheboth Gebiet to settle them. This proved a failure and quarrels ensued. The remaining members of the group then crossed over into Angola where in the southern parts I met some of their blond, tall, Afrikaans-speaking descendants. Others returned since to the Republic; others yet intermarried with the Portuguese.

We landed just in time near Swakopmund before the fog became impenetrable. This is one of the strangest places I ever saw. The first German settlement, this coastal town appears like a combination of a pre-1914 Baltic resort place, and a ghost town of the American Far West. Sandy streets, with buildings in a turn-of-the-century style, which used to be hotels in the high-living days, stand now empty, looking with blind windows towards the desert or the ocean. Other buildings, low one-story structures, reminiscent of midwestern American main streets, have active shops and the waterfront has a range of well-frequented hotels. As everywhere in South West Africa, and as in America, the inhabitants, native and newcomers, proudly show the visitor the old and the new, anxiously watching the reaction on his face.

About a half-hour's drive from Swakopmund is Walvis Bay, the town and the four-hundred-square-mile territory excised from the body of South West Africa, and annexed by the British in 1878. Now it is part of the Republic of South Africa, but is administered like the rest from Windhoek. Walvis Bay is the most active part of South West Africa, and it is expanding rapidly over the dunes. In fact, it is built on dunes, which are specially treated to make them solid; then one may build on them just as on firm ground.

Since this is the industrial and business center of the country, even more than Windhoek, because it has a large and accommodating port, it was interesting to hear business leaders speak of the future. Like South West Africans elsewhere, but with more articulation, they have the pioneer state of mind. They, the director of fisheries, or of the port authority, reminded me of American businessmen, full of confidence and plans. Their biggest problem is to break out of the limitations that nature and distance impose on South West Africa; underpopulation is in the way of developing resources and establishing active centers of light industry. The scarcity of local customers compels the industries to sell their products either to the Republic or overseas. But transportation and shipping costs are high, although the fisheries do an excellent business. In spite of the handicaps, new firms settle in Windhoek in expensive tall buildings whose neon advertisements compete with a voraciously red sky. And tall buildings in Windhoek indicate prosperity in Walvis Bay and vice versa. High quality crayfish, shrimp, and fish meal are welcome the world over; those countries which join in the futile and hypocritical game of boycotting South West African products pay slightly more per can of sea food since they buy through middle men under various labels.

Walvis Bay is perhaps the best place to stop and ask the reader to join my investigation of the black contract workers' living conditions. There are of course differences in this respect and it would be incorrect to assume, for example, that the near-luxurious conditions prevailing in the very rich Oranjemund Diamond mines are duplicated elsewhere. But it would be equally incorrect to give credit to Mr. Allard K. Löwenstein's words when he speaks of the natives' "weary, quicksand struggle to fend off starvation and to avoid being beaten or jailed for another day."*

It is, of course, regrettable that the United Nations establishes its reports on such statements, because investigations showing the contrary appear then similarly exag-

* *Brutal Mandate: A Journey to South West Africa,* foreword by Mrs. Franklin D. Roosevelt. Macmillan, New York.

gerated. But unfortunately, it is the effect of untrue and tendentious reporting that at least some of it sticks in some minds and any reasoned refutation seems like an effort at whitewashing.

Whether it is Tsumeb, Walvis Bay, Luderitz, Windhoek, Oranjemund or elsewhere, the African working out his contract period in the Police Zone without his family, lives in a compound built either by the company he works for, or by the municipality. There are usually six men to a room, which has the characteristics of a dormitory: beds, tables, lockers, shelves; often sewing machines, or some other means of doing personal work in spare time. As far as food is concerned, I have never seen greater care given to meals prepared for large numbers of people, either in student cafeterias in the United State or Europe, or in hospitals, or even in middle class restaurants. I realized with stupefaction yet another aspect of the South Africans' systematic methods. Clean kitchens have modern equipment for cutting meat, boiling vegetables, tapping beer, dispensing tea, distributing cakes or pies. At the entrance is a typed menu of the day, with mention of calories and the exact quantity of every ingredient. Particular care is taken to offer varied and tasty meals; in Walvis Bay, for example, there are fourteen menus worked out so that the same dish cannot appear on the table more than twice a month.

If Mr. Löwenstein, impelled by ideological motives, and in search of adventure, had not chosen to undertake a clandestine trip into South West Africa, he would have seen all this, although it is an unanswered question whether or not he would have admitted anything so favorable in his report. But he chose not to see, with the result that his discoveries, fed into eager United Nations' ears would make the entire continent of Africa laugh. For example, he states that the natives "live with disease, subsisting on a diet whose mainstay is a tasteless porridge called 'mealy meal'." (Page 79) If Mr. Löwenstein had taken the trouble of asking an African he could have found out that 1) mealy meal is the most popular food-stuff all over black Africa; 2) the whites eat it in large quantities; 3) long efforts by whites have not succeeded in persuading blacks everywhere to eat a balanced diet; and 4) the compounds I described above, while serving mealy meal on general request, have succeeded, as indicated above, practically in imposing variety, vitamins, and adequate calories. Every company has doctors for its workers who check up regularly on health conditions.

The work period never exceeds eight hours, since most companies work three shifts. I visited compounds at any hour of the day, and witnessed the men either sleeping or at the following occupations: cleaning themselves; doing their personal laundry; drinking beer; playing soccer; attending movies; doing odd jobs in a specially provided workshop equipped for sewing, carpentry, shoe repair, or sandal making. Others were putting on clean shirts and ties, were leaving the compound to take a stroll or visit friends (and girl friends) in the native township.

The townships themselves follow the pattern of those in the Republic. One may disagree with the whole concept of separate development, and deplore the fact of racial friction, not only in South Africa, but in almost all

AFRICA

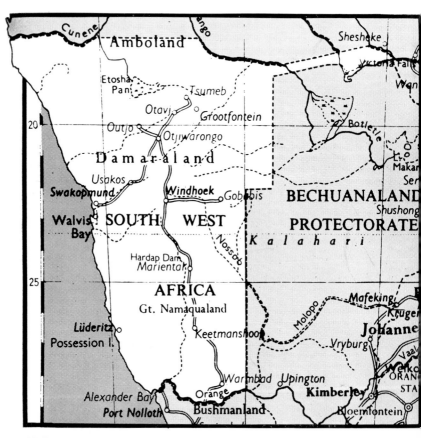

SOUTH WEST AFRICA (South African Information Service)

Windhoek Airport (S.A.I.S.)

Administration Building, Windhoek (S.A.I.S.)

Windhoek, Castle (S.A.I.S.)

Opening of Provincial Administration Building, Windhoek (S.A.I.S.)

Mr. Paul Kruger, one of the Bantu Affairs Commissioners in life-long service of native well-being and progress. (Photos by Carin Molnar)

The kraal is the native farmer's home and castle. The concentric fencing helps trap the stray wild animals which are attracted by the cattle inside.

A lonely gaze over the South Atlantic.

Near Luderitz thousands of seals play, swim, make love, fight duels—and become fur coats at a later stage. (Photo by Carin Molnar)

This strapping fellow is Jakob, a young penguin.

Our pilot has a good grip. Later, we let the young desert fox run. (Photos by Carin Molnar)

Lobster Canning Factory, Luderitz (S.A.I.S.)

Fishmeal Factory, Luderitz (S.A.I.S.)

Karakul Industry (S.A.I.S.)

Karakul Sheep (S.A.I.S.)

Gemstone Dealer, Windhoek (S.A.I.S.)

Native Handicrafts at Grootfontein (S.A.I.S.)

Agricultural workers at Vunga-Vunga (S.A.I.S.)

Marble Works, Karibib (S.A.I.S.)

Rehoboth Woman (S.A.I.S.)

Bantu Beauty Parade, Swakopmund (S.A.I.S.)

Ruth Walter, Sculptress in Wood, Gobabis (S.A.I.S.)

Chocolate Factory, Windhoek (S.A.I.S.)

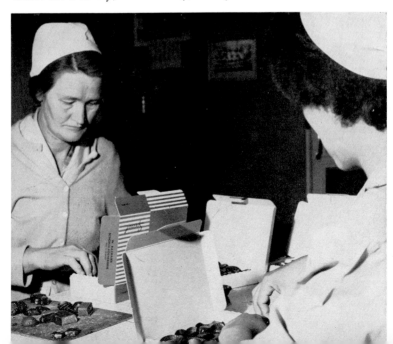

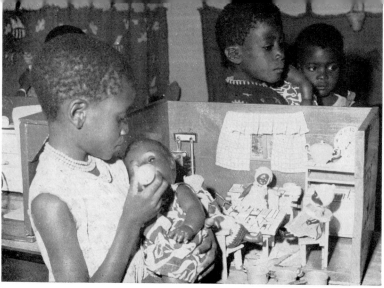

Mission Kindergarten at Karibib (S.A.I.S.)

Teachers Training School, Ovamboland (S.A.I.S.)

School in Windhoek (S.A.I.S.)

Baster School, Rehoboth (S.A.I.S.)

Hospital at Oshakati, Ovamboland (S.A.I.S.)

Medical Care in Ovamboland (S.A.I.S.)

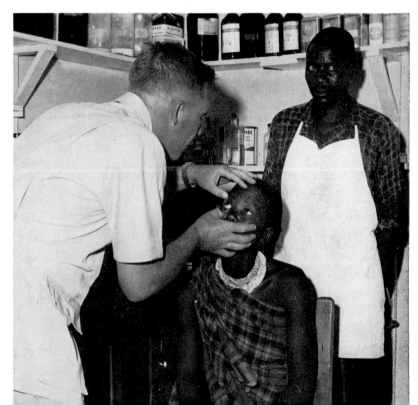

parts of the world, but the line must be drawn when critics denounce the native townships as concentration camps. In South West Africa, like the Republic of South Africa, postwar industrial boom has attracted tens of thousands of Africans to the new urban and work centers. The version presented by South Africa's systematic denigrators is once more untrue. They assert that a diabolical plan was hatched in the white man's mind. The natives were deprived of their cultivable land, so that in the despair of poverty they were forced to offer their work to the white men, and accept starving wages in place of greater misery. This is, of course, Mr. Löwenstein's thesis too.

Reality, as I suggested above, shows the magnetic appeal of western and urban ways of life, sufficient in every part of the world to attract the rural population. Right after 1945 the working men had no other choice but to crowd into dreadful slums, where they and their families became easy victims of slumlords, gangs, and of the wares that both categories were plying: alcohol, drugs, prostitution. This was true of the large cities in South Africa, Johannesburg, Durban, Port Elizabeth, or of the smaller urban concentrations in the South West. This dismal situation lasted for about fifteen years; since about 1960, the government in cooperation with the municipalities, has undertaken the relocation and the rehabilitation of the slum population. New townships were built, which may look gloomily uniform from a distance, but which show variety, green areas, and individuality at close range.

One would think that the compressed population was

happy to exchange the old pace for the new, healthy and well-policed one. Generally this was the case. But not always and everywhere, for the following reason: The slumlords who used to exploit every square inch in order to draw more rent were confronted with obvious losses. Not only did they lose their "regular" revenues, but also the above-mentioned illicit, but highly profitable, trade. Before the law, they were powerless; but through gangs, with which they shared profits, they could exert a pressure on at least part of the inhabitants. Many of the latter just refused to leave, and yielded only to police intervention. There was no question of anybody remaining in the old slums which were slated to be burned down and put to better use as industrial areas, public gardens, or, indeed, new townships. The usually hostile segment of the western press published photographs of the cases of forcible population transfer, and took up at once the cry of "police state"; or its reporters claimed to have witnessed a desperate resistance to "wholesale transportation to concentration camps."*

These events date back now to about a decade, but the reports at present sound a similar "alarm" over native townships in South West Africa. Here progress is generally slower than in the Republic, and the townships are still being built, in some cases only planned as yet. Let me

---

* This reminds me of some other reportorial feats of objectivity. In Salisbury, after independence, western reporters, who shall remain unnamed, had the habit of throwing a few coins into public garbage cans, then took pictures of black children rushing to take them out. The caption under the photographs read, "Starved Native Children Rummage for Food Remains Among the Refuse."

mention three of them, which will give an adequate description of what is being done.

The largest and a beautiful one is Katutura, near Windhoek. While visiting it and ascertaining the real situation *de visu*, I was reading articles in the western press describing it in the same stereotyped terms that home editors do not even bother to change from one reportorial "revelation" to the next. Thus, Katutura was described as located in the most unfavorable part of the area, as being flat and unattractive, as being overcrowded, as being heavily guarded by white police and fenced in "camp style."

It was also mentioned, but this must have been copied from the local Windhoek opposition newspaper, that many of the homes stayed empty because the population of the older township refuses to move in (obviously in fear of police brutality and concentration camp living conditions).

My observation is, Katutura, like the entire Windhoek region, is picturesque and is not flat, but hilly, like Windhoek. The houses, like those in Luderitz and elsewhere, are painted in different colors so as to avoid uniformity, and overcrowding is strictly forbidden to the point that the number of alien lodgers is limited to one. Police of course exist, but I never saw a city in any part of the world without them; based on previous experience in the early locations, this is certainly a blessing. A fence runs alongside the highway, preventing children and domestic animals from being overrun by cars and other vehicles. I repeat that I visited every section of this new town and found assembly and concert halls, movie theaters, post office and bank, well-stocked stores, and a public library. If all this be mere façade to serve the purpose of hiding and disguising the places where police brutality never stops and the victims of terror cry to heaven, then I must say it is an expensive façade and a most fantastically skillful stage setting involving the participation of thousands of actors.

Out of the eight thousand homes of Katutura, some fifteen hundred are still unoccupied. Why? The reason is the above-characterized intimidation: a combination of gang dictatorship, political agitation, and as always in Africa, the influence of the witch doctor. But perhaps direct threat is the most effective of the three: Families who wish to move to the clean homes of Katutura find strips of papers under their door; "If you move, we cut your throat!"*

Near Katutura there is an even better-looking township for the Coloured, most of whom are from the Rehoboth Gebiet, south of Windhoek. Another Coloured township is in Walvis Bay, where I visited the school and was guided around by its young Coloured principal. Here I noted

---

* I have read, in the World Court dossier of the South West Africa case, copies of letters by Mr. Getsen, a South African nationalist petitioner at the United Nations, urging his home-based fellows to prevent the population of Windhoek's native location from moving into the clean, well-laid-out houses of the brand-new Katutura township. Why this fear of seeing infinitely better living conditions for thousands of families? Possibly because people living in pleasant surroundings are not amenable to supplying revolutionary shock troops? Mr. Getsen apparently both hopes to exploit discontent with the present location, and also incite the United Nations against Pretoria, which supposedly keeps them there.

something I never saw before: kindergarten children have a section of the building for themselves, with lower ceilings, and lower wash basins, etc., a kind of miniaturized world. The architect really thought of everything. This is the more remarkable, since like everything in Walvis Bay, it shows that practical mentality, functionalism, and immediate usefulness take precedence over considerations of comfort. Everything is still unfinished; wide areas where residences for parks are planned are still exposed to sun and wind, and the busses of the coloured township cross half-a-mile between one block of buildings and the next.

While Walvis Bay had the money to develop its two townships, one for Africans, the other for Coloured, Luderitz, further south on the coast, offers the example of a poor, but valiantly struggling, community in need of state loans for its own townships. Like Swakopmund, Luderitz is among the earliest German settlements, and like the former, it is predominantly German-speaking. It is built on an extremely rocky terrain, isolated from the interior, suffering from a scarcity of drinking and irrigation water.

The psychology of pioneer towns is that they try to do everything at the same time. In the case of Luderitz, this compulsion takes moving and fervent forms, in the words of its mayor, a native of Germany, and the director of the fisheries, a second generation German. Both reminded me of a similar class of Americans, especially in their faith in the future of this God-forsaken-looking rocky outpost, destined to become in their eyes, a major port, a summer resort, and a center of industry. They were proudest of the new hospital for natives (a far more modern and better equipped one than the old hospital for whites), and particularly of the Coloured and African townships. Special care had been taken to paint the houses different pastel shades so as to preserve their individuality.

In spite of the Luderitz officials' ambitious vision, I could not suppress the sensation of being at the end of the world. To be sure we had arrived at this styleless town on a Saturday night and found nobody on the streets. In fact, these were not even streets but throughways between haphazardly-built, scattered houses. Maybe pioneer souls find in all this a challenge; for me Luderitz seemed like the last barren rock before icy nothingless. I thought that Patagonia might be similar.

This underlying impression may have been created by our visit that afternoon to the dwelling place of the seals a few miles to the north of Luderitz. This was one of the most extraordinary experiences. First of all on arrival at the by now usual grassy landing strip, we were taken in charge and driven in a Land Rover through a town, property of the C.D.M. (diamond mines), but abandoned several years ago as a no-longer-usable area. The strange thing is that C.D.M. rules forbid any furniture to be removed from the ex-homes, because they may be hiding diamonds. Thus the place is today a ghost town and looks as if life had been suddenly interrupted in it, and the inhabitants forced to flee without their belongings, somewhat like an industrial Pompeii.

The Land Rover began to scale what appeared from afar as unscalable rocks. Suddenly the sea wind blew a penetrating stench in our direction and the rocks showed traces of dried blood. We were in what I can only describe as a town of seals; between us, appearing like invaders from another planet, and the ocean with its rough, high waves, there was a rocky terrain pinkish with layers of blood, and teeming with thousands of seals! From enormous and bellowing bulls to small (25 pound ?) bleating babies, seals everywhere, brownish-black, dragging themselves heavily, playing in the water, taking enormous leaps through mountainous waves. We realized now that the stench came from the corpses of dead bulls, fallen in grim duels over the females and slowly consumed at nightfall by stealthy jackals. We realized also that our presence had thrown the rocks' clumsy citizens into great agitation; seal mothers were calling their little ones, which were desperately trying to reach the shelter of the sea. There, *we* would be at a disadvantage. Others, not being able to make it, chose to hide among the rocks; my wife claims that a particularly smart baby seal pretended sleep, and opened one suspicious eye as she passed. I am told he even winked.

Seals form Luderitz' second source of revenue besides crayfish. Fortunately we were spared the sight of seals bludgeoned to death by tannery workers, who then skin them. But even without witnessing that sacrifice on the altar of feminine elegance, the seals' rock provided us with enough drama. The hours spent there certainly colored my impressions for the next day or two.

CHAPTER 4

ROADS TO THE FUTURE

W HO WOULD not be interested in visiting a diamond
mine? The word "mine" is associated with subterranean excavations, unhealthy conditions, the breath-
ing of heavy dust. Yet "diamond" changes the word into
something pure, hard and clean, and one does not imagine
diamond miners covered with dirt and straining with
effort.

South Africa is the world's foremost producer of diamonds, and half the coastal strip of South West Africa
forms a concession to the Oppenheimer Corporation for
the excavation of that precious stone. Like California in
1849, this territory too used to be the dreamland for
thousands who expected to derive from it quick and easy
fortunes. Under German rule, the mining of diamonds
continued with laughably primitive methods: rows of
workers crawling, or on their knees, were scanning and
sifting the sand and turning up occasional bright pebbles.
In a way, the same method is utilized now, only instead of

crawling men, there are enormous bulldozer-like machines, which remove layer after layer of sand, until they reach the diamondiferous soil.

The surprise that Oranjemund provides is not the nature of its mining, which is almost casual, but the oasis created by the company in the middle of a sandy desert. The company town stands as a striking monument to what ingeniosity and organization can achieve in even the most adverse conditions. Money of course helps; company revenues even after sizable taxes are enough to establish a model settlement, lovely homes, gardens, farms, with hothouse fruit and vegetables, abundant shopping centers. In the last chapter I have described the workers' compound which makes Oranjemund a much-sought-for work place. The four thousand black employees return faithfully after each interruption of the contract period. If they return within a year, they begin work on the basis of the last-received wages.

As elsewhere, wages and work should not be discussed separately from the overall picture of the black man's situation. Yet this is the most difficult aspect to convey to the reader, who is not familiar with the situation, but who is often offered tendentious presentations. And for a presentation to be tendentious, and sow erroneous ideas into ears which are usually only half-listening anyway, it is enough simply to apply western concepts and criteria in describing non-western situations.

South West Africa is a pioneer country, slowly opened up for development. It is roughly in the position of the American West of a hundred years ago. The decisive difference is that the Americans treated the indigenous population, the Indians, as a nation half conquered and partly to be still conquered; at any rate, as an adversary whose fate, however, was not in doubt. It had to yield to superior force, numbers, know-how, and wile.

In South West Africa, the whites, on the contrary, have been and will be a minority, and they have never envisaged nor can envisage the subjugation of the native population. For a number of decades, under German colonial status, the situation could have been described as stagnating. The Germans, often with rough methods, had put an end to the tribes' mutual extermination campaigns, and settled down to develop the territory, first of all the coast, but also, to lesser extent, the interior.

Germans and South Africans alike have understood one thing, the thing that all colonizers knew in Africa: The black population, in every instance the majority, must be brought gradually into the modern world, through means suited to the nature of the problem. Each colonizing empire approached this task in a different manner, but evidence shows today that each failed, very probably because they had never really intended to prolong their colonial rule on a permanent basis. Proof of this is that when equalitarian ideologies swept the world after 1945, and the question of racial integration could no longer be avoided, one after the other the European colonizers preferred to withdraw from the continent. The excuses they gave were of diverse nature, they even clothed their withdrawal in the garb of high morality; yet when the question arose in all its nakedness whether Paris ought to enter in agreement of dual citizenship with the black and Arab states of the French ex-empire, General De Gaulle brutally cut the ties of the Communauté, rather than see France inundated by millions of coloured men.

The same thing is taking place in England, that is, in another country where work opportunities attract colored individuals from the commonwealth nations. But both Conservative and Labor governments had agreed tacitly, and translated their agreement into law, that such a colored invasion would gradually alter, if not destroy, the white western character of their people, a way of life, and civilization. Hence, the strict limits imposed on nonwhite immigration.

The policy pursued by South Africa in the former mandate territory must be viewed in the same light, although the situation is naturally complicated by a number of factors which neither Paris nor London had to take into consideration. On the continent of Africa the blacks are and will remain in majority. Yet, only the most primitive of democrats would say that this is a sufficient reason to plunge the country into the deepest misery; a saner view will suggest that the black majority ought to be developed in contact with white civilization, but without depriving it of the characteristics which will forge it into nations.

Again only the ideologically oriented would deny that the plans for future nationhood must be laid, and the initial impetus toward it given by the whites. This is what happened in the decolonized territories also; the whites drew the boundary lines of the present black states; the whites created the institutions of the new states, drew up their constitutions and provided the models for their laws; trained the personnel in whatever number, laid the economic foundations, imposed the work habits. To this day, and in spite of the repeated upheavals, the new countries still bear the white man's impact.

There should be then no objection if South Africa performs the same functions in South West Africa (and through the Bantustan policy, in the Republic, too). Moreover, it should be realized that dealing with a distinct race and the majority at that, it is preferable to bring it collectively to the threshold of nationhood than divide it into contending classes of intellectuals, bourgeois, leaders, workers, each sufficiently ideologized to prepare the class struggle and paralyze the state when it finally comes into existence. This explains why Pretoria does not detach talented or otherwise exceptional members of a tribe and plunge them into a white milieu as evolués, but pumps them back, as it were, into the tribe so that they may serve the communal progress of the entire future nation.

This policy is certainly distasteful to individualistic white men, and particularly to Americans. But let us make the effort of seeing the specific character of every civilization and nation. The United States became the world's most powerful country by creaming off the most enterprising elements of each nation in Europe. Consequently, it may appear quite hopeless to persuade Americans, all of them of immigrant stock, that the best methods for collective success is not the extension of opportunities to the most daring and enterprising members of a community.

Yet the South Africans answer by recalling their own experiences in nation-building, and in being an African nation; the Afrikaner element argues that in order to overcome discrimination by the British in the nineteenth century and the first half of the twentieth, it first forged an Afrikaner consciousness, then stormed the citadel of British privileges as a united, national, and linguistic community. Why should not the black tribes too become nations in the same way, that is, through a feeling of cohesion and recognition of being a distinct entity?

The contrary approach shows, in the irrefutable argument of the South Africans, that by detaching the elite of the black nations, the colonizers trained them not according to African realities, but in the political and ideological spirit of Europe and America. What was the use, Pretoria asks now, of making British- and French-style gentlemen and statesmen out of an Abubakar Tafewa Balewa, an Nkrumah, a Sekou Touré (plus the political class around them) when they could not thus be successfully reabsorbed by their communities; they either became gesticulating revolutionaries or public figures with distorted contemporary-white concepts under their black skins. In either case, they represent something alien to the African milieu; the explosion must, and indeed does occur sooner or later. Irreconcilable elements have been forced to fuse in an impossible formula.

The South African way, however shocking at first sight to those immersed in western experience, has many things to recommend it, among them a contrast to the negative and disastrous experience elsewhere on the continent. In discussing this "way" we should of course have South West Africa in mind; but since the laws applied there have been tested in the Republic, any discussion or prospects for black development in South West Africa must take into consideration what the more advanced degree of development in South Africa has so far achieved, and what it is scheduled to achieve. These plans, as far as South West Africa is concerned, have been worked out by the so-called Odendaal commission, which made detailed recommendations in a report in 1963. Pretoria considers it as the blueprint for South West African development; it contains therefore the indications of official policy.

The Odendaal Report can only be understood on the basis of past history, the present African situation, and the present degree of development of the black population. These factors impose upon the reader the obligation of putting his preferences and abstract ideals aside, and of looking exclusively at concrete reality.

Although petitioners before the United Nations prefer to denounce the white man's atrocities only, and as a rule begin by quoting instances of German brutality, there remains inseparable from the history of South West Africa the fact of attempted mutual extermination by the tribes long before the white man appeared there. Particularly in the light of present day conflicts between the constituent tribal, racial, ethnic and religious elements of each black or Arab African state, South Africa cannot envisage a policy urged by the petitioners of working toward a unitary and unified national state in South West Africa. Were this done, one can be sure, on the basis of available evidence, that the various black nations would first turn against the white minority, blaming it for troubles past and present, and would ultimately eliminate it as an alien, uncooperative element obstructing real unity. But the next phase would see the falling out of the black tribes among themselves and the revival of the old conflicts with modern weapons!

"Separate development," however distasteful a connotation the term has acquired in certain minds, seems therefore the only alternative to 1) present South African rule over the entire territory, or 2) the chaos of an artificially unified state. The main overriding task is therefore to prevent wholesale detribalization (hence the contract system) while encouraging the simultaneous development of the homelands.

We have argued for the prevention of detribalization and against the forced integration of two communities, black and white, both strong enough (one through its numbers and specific culture, the other through the awareness and defense of its achievements) to create perpetual friction between them.*

Let us now see the problems the black development poses. In reading the Odendaal report, one realizes today (in 1966) that it has incorporated most of the work that had been done before the Commission had been set up,

* Whatever we think of the integration issue in the United States, we must keep in mind that there is no parallel between the American and African situation. In the latter the black community simply cannot be absorbed by the white, and the white community by the black. Moreover, while the United States Negro has long ago been "Americanized" the African black man will never adopt white ways, thinking, and methods. And why should he?

and also the work in progress while the Commission was studying the problem. So that traveling in South West Africa, the Report may almost serve as a guidebook of what one can see now and what to expect to see in the future.

The first new proposal contained in the Report is the increase of the native territory. Past migrations have resulted in a rather patchy map of South West Africa, because various tribes and subtribes, in pursuit of grazing land and water, became scattered. This is, by the way, the same in the territory of the Republic. Nations like Zulu, Xhosa, Tswana, Venda, Swasi, Basuto, Bechuana, etc., have settled in the course of their history in various parts of the subcontinent. And we witness now the process set in motion partly by the South Africans, partly by the British in their three protectorates, of granting self-rule to these national entities, after rounding out their territories.

The present total area of the homeland will be increased by about a third. The gain will be made up from government land, game reserves (an excellent source of tourist revenue), and hundreds of white-owned farms bought up by the government and handed over as black property. Question and controversy here regard the quality of soil and resources of existing homelands, and of the territories they are scheduled to gain. Petitioners argue that Pretoria, after having pushed the black tribes into hardly accessible and poor areas, intends now to turn over to them similarly unproductive land. First it should be acknowledged that Ovamboland, for example, and generally the north, with the exception of Kaokoveld, is the most fertile land in otherwise stony, sandy, and rocky South West Africa, and that it receives the largest quantity of rainfall. Then, as the government points out, what would be the purpose of turning over to an overwhelmingly rural, agricultural population, factories, and mines for which it lacks know-how and capital to exploit.

This seems like circular reasoning, and one may assume that once self-rule is granted, further negotiations will render the presently-envisaged policy more elastic. For the time being Pretoria argues that the entire South West Africa must be developed to the limits of its capacity and this can only be done by white investment, organization, and knowledge. Mines, factories, and industries established anywhere in the territory help the entire population directly, through work opportunity and acquired skills and services, such as medical care, education, veterinary care, etc.

The great majority of the population, expressing its will through the chiefs, approves the policy of developing the homelands in this fashion. Only one tribe refuses to co-operate, the Herero, the same one whose existence was threatened by total extinction by the Namas in the course of the nineteenth century. It is proverbial in South West Africa that the Hereros are the most aggressive and quarrelsome nation, the ones whose mention calls wry smiles and often insulting remarks to the lips of others.

It is usually argued in liberal circles that the chiefs do not represent anybody except their own privileged status, itself sustained only through the authority of the whites. The world is told that the chiefs are a backward class, uneducated and uneducable; when they are old, they are represented as senile, when young as irresponsible play-boys. General African experience does not bear this out at all, but then Africa is oftentimes seen through the distorting lens of radicalism. By contrast, it is strange that when we read the petitioners' testimony before the United Nations, suddenly some traditional chiefs of South West Africa leap into evidence, simply, one gathers, because this time they are opposed to Pretoria's policies. But one needs choose one of two things: either the chiefs are reliable judges of their people's interests, and those among them who favor the separate development policy do so responsibly and not as the "white man's stooges"—or they are ignorant, senile, and dishonest, in which case their messages to the United Nations are not worth serious consideration. That some of them, given the corruptibility of human nature, are instruments of white decisions I do not know, but would not be surprised if it were true. What is one to think, however, of one of the refugee petitioners, Mr. Getsen, who in a letter from abroad to a member of his movement instructed him to enlist the chiefs' support, by granting them, like candy to children, high-sounding titles in the organization; President, First Vice-President, Second, Third, etc. Vice-President.*

I suggest that the controversy over the chiefs' representability cannot be settled by some gratuitous verdict against them. South Africa is on the record that it considers the chiefs and the populations under their adminis-

---

* From the testimony at The Hague by Mr. Kurt Dahlmann, editor of the Windhoek "*Allgemeine Zeitung.*"

tration, with the exception of the Bushmen, who have no chiefs or political structure, as having reached the stage where a larger measure of self-government can be entrusted to them. Accordingly the Odendaal Report suggests that the existing native authorities of the homelands be transformed into "full-fledged legislative councils," for which additional members (that is, in addition to the chiefs and headmen) should be elected by popular franchise. An executive committee elected from the council members would be vested with the executive power. The legislative council would consist of the presently functioning authority, namely three chiefs and thirty-two headmen, with as many additional members elected as commensurate with the number of votes in a given area. Initially, the number of elected members would not constitute more than forty percent of the council, so that democratic methods of suffrage might have some time to mature and become practicable.

The Legislative Council in Ovamboland, for example is scheduled to take over gradually from the department of Bantu administration such legislative and administrative functions that the latter possesses. Eventually, the Legislative Council will possess full functions, except defense, foreign affairs, general security, water power generation, and so on.

The next step will be the introduction of homeland citizenship. Men and women above eighteen years of age would be granted voting rights in their respective homelands.

One can see from these recommendations, and they

represent official government policy, that the same orderly evolution is planned for the homelands, starting with Ovamboland, as for the Bantustans now being set up in the Republic of South Africa. In a way, their establishment will be less arduous than that of the Bantustans. First, because there are many fewer, even comparatively, Ovambo in the Police Zone than Bantu in the various South African urban areas; secondly, because South West Africa's white population favors, in its majority, this solution, whereas it took more than a decade to persuade the South African electorate to agree to and finance the Bantustan policy. The end result is encouraging. The road to self-rule and future complete independence is outlined, and the first signposts are set up; those who argue that a South West African black man looks to a hopeless future for himself and his children are wrong; it is in the nature of political bodies, that once set up, even in rudimentary forms, their evolution becomes incalculable. A multitude of Ovambo or Nama can and will find satisfaction in the kind of self-ruled homeland now being set up for and by them.

There will still remain a large number of natives migrating to the Police Zone for work. This, however, represents no continuing form of compulsory labor, as the petitioners and other critics maintain. This form of migratory labor will remain in existence as long as the native territories are not able to absorb their own manpower, which is to say for a long time. The same is true of the ex-British protectorates, Basotuland, Swaziland, and Bechuanaland, whose respective prime ministers have made it clear that their economic future is tied up with that of South Africa. This includes not only the sale to South Africa of their cattle and agricultural products, but also the presence in the Republic of their surplus population capable to work.

Natives residing in the Police Zone will see their rights and responsibilities increase. The legislative councils operating in the homelands will nominate a member of the urban councils, with representational powers. This is again in imitation of the Bantustan policy and helps the weight both of the homeland authorities and of their racial brothers residing in the Police Zone.

Political development must be underlined by progress of the economy. Here again, one should begin with a comparison between South West Africa's present and prospects, and the sorry state of most new countries on the continent. It is no secret any more that part, perhaps a major part, of the chronic political instability in these countries is due to the disastrous economic policy of their ruling class. This is not the place to analyze the ideological basis for most of the economic decisions taken in many African countries today; nor is it possible to explain here the causes of other deficiencies and incompetences. The facts, nevertheless, remain incontrovertible: The leaders of emerging countries wreck their economies by 1) eliminating the still crucially important white presence from ownership and management positions; 2) launching prestige projects with no relevance to resources, needs, and carrying capacity of these countries; 3) pressing for an impossible industrialization for the sake of obtaining spectacular aid from abroad; 4) socializing the economy under a corrupt and inefficient party bureaucracy; 5) yielding to ideological bias by creating at an exorbitant expense, Soviet- or Chinese-type farms and factories, the kind which are dismal failures in Communist lands, but help shine the revolutionary label abroad.*

The chief critics and most aggressive denunciators of South Africa in its South West African policies are the socialists and Communists. Partly because, one gathers, Pretoria applies a modest but sane economic policy within the capabilities of its budget, although at times straining it to the limit. South Africa had contributed 300 rand per capita in aid to the well-being of South West Africa, the kind of foreign aid not easily matched by other powers extending aid to African countries. But this aid is not spectacular; it does not result in steel mills in the middle of Ovamboland, nor will it result in the manufacture of atomic bombs, as American aid does in India, a country in desperate need of even enough bowls of rice.

The economic development of the homelands is planned according to the needs of the population and the

* When the dictator Kwame Nkrumah fell in Ghana, it was found that state farms on Soviet model were run at enormous deficits for years, but were considered sacred and above criticism by the regime. This is what *The New York Times,* one-time friend and supporter of Nkrumah, had to admit on March 3, 1966: "In Ghana, from a practical viewpoint, many communist aid programs were inefficient, costly and often un-necessary to the Ghanaian economy. For example, Ghana put three times more money into the six Soviet sponsored state farms than the value of the farms' produce." *The New York Times* a few years ago editorially argued that although Dr. Nkrumah (now the fallen despot has been demoted to "Mister") voted with the communist bloc in the United Nations and was clearly anti-American, Washington ought to support him and grant him the aid he requests for building a new dam.

resources of the territory. The territory in question is not just the homeland which would be unable to provide for itself adequately, let alone invest in its future, but the entire South West Africa aided by the Republic. And this is a correct thing, since native labor contributes in turn to the development of South West Africa. I have noted during my travels that among underdeveloped countries only those prosper and look forward to progress which live within their means, and put foreign aid to intelligent use. Ivory Coast in Africa, and Taiwan in Asia come to my mind, because these countries have understood the essential rule of underdevelopment: genuine help to the agricultural population and the establishment of industries in conjunction with agricultural resources and the needs of farmers. Taiwan especially serves as a model in this respect. The local industries help farmers market their produce (for example, canning factories) and help them again with items they need and can afford; farm equipment, bicycles, sewing machines.

The same considerations hold with regard to the development of the homelands. The Police Zone is generally rocky, desert land, which must import most of its food requirements from the Republic. If Ovamboland and the Okavango can be developed, their frequent cattle diseases stemmed, and the quantity and quality of the crop improved through irrigation, then the north may become a substantial supplier of the rest of the territory. The Odendaal Report suggests the setting up of a livestock producers' trust, a slaughtering and marketing concern, meat processing plants, and canneries. In the southern homelands where the climate is dry and the annual rainfall low, experimental farms are established and the further breeding of karakul sheep is encouraged.

These resources will allow small and gradual moves toward secondary industries, using timber, jute, and other natural products. What primary industry exists needs the presence of the white population to exploit the mines and run the factories and fisheries. They in turn contribute to the well-being of the northern and southern sections in the form of cash wages and community services in addition to what the state provides, using their tax money. Thus any removal of the white minority (about 15% of the total population figure) would paralyze the territory's development and expose it to vicissitudes possibly worse than what other African countries now experience. Realism suggests then that while each national unit must evolve toward its best specific national objectives, economically South West Africa must be considered as a unit, each coexisting race or nation assisting the overall development according to its own ability.

This in turn raises the question of cultural evolution in general, problems of health and schooling in particular. The question has its importance also because the petitioners accuse South Africa of practicing a policy of extermination of the natives or of allowing various diseases to decimate them and ignorance to remain unrelieved among them. The councils of the United Nations listen in full earnestness to denunciations such as this: Instead of curing disease-affected herds, South African officials spread sickness so as to have a pretext for killing cattle wholesale! Concerning human beings, the same nonsense is repeated endlessly: tens of thousands live in squalor, suffering from infectious diseases which supposedly carry them away at an early age since they are undernourished!

When the petitioners, after telling their horror stories, come to the problem of education, they have an easy time. Who would believe that such exploited human beings, starved and beaten with the sjambok, would be given any instruction at all by their cruel masters? The version that is spread is that native children are either not educated at all, or when some semblance of effort is made in the direction of lifting some of them from abysmal ignorance, this is done with guile: They are expected to learn in their own language, never in English, so as to prevent their contact with the outside world, and apparently prevent them also from becoming petitioners. Mr. Löwenstein is eager to present native education too as a sham. Course work, he writes, is modeled on the system already in force in the Union. It consists of such items as handicraft, nature study, hygiene, and religion.

Let us then tackle again the topic of well-being among the tribes. An objective traveler will testify that he has not seen underfed or disease-ridden blacks in South West Africa, as he inevitably will while visiting other African countries. In the public squares and streets of the latter, after years of independence, horribly diseased and deformed legions will beg him for alms, and he will also walk among miserable huts while the country's new elite live in beautiful villas and drive in expensive automobiles.

Even in Nigeria, for years held up as a model of British-style administration, it was found after the January, 1966, coup that the finance minister, massacred together with other leaders, had a Swiss bank account with 15 million dollars put aside. Reports have it that he tearfully offered some of it to the assassins who had invaded his home in the middle of the night. Newspaper accounts stated that he pleaded, "I give you one million, no, two millions," without succeeding in softening their hearts or offering enough.

While some tropical diseases have made the beginning of a comeback in certain parts of independent Africa, for example, in the Congo, the South African authorities have successfully fought all of them and would be completely successful if, as I learned in the eastern Caprivi, the natives did not wait with their visit to the hospital until the last minute or beyond. I saw several such cases (sleeping sickness still takes a toll) being treated. Malaria is perhaps the most tenacious of these diseases. Authorities in Ovamboland finally persuaded the natives to accept periodic spraying of their huts with DDT, but until recently this was considered by the witch doctors as a dangerous interference with their own work; they incited the population with charges that the whites' "powder" spreads disease among people and beasts. When finally the sprayings began, the villagers gratefully admitted that for the first time it was possible to spend a quiet night in their huts. In one of the huts over 900 dead mosquitoes were found after spraying.

Infantile mortality used to be 60 to 70% before the

arrival of the white man in South West Africa. It is now reduced to 10%, as witnessed by the growth of the population. The only sickness still a problem is tuberculosis, according to the doctors. It is attacked not only with modern medicines, but primarily through prevention: isolation of the sick, but mostly through the introduction of a healthier diet.

The consequent population increase over the past decade poses the problem of training more teachers and building more schools. The reader does not have to be told that this shortage is acute today everywhere in the world. Yet only the South Africans are held up and accused of a sinister conspiracy against the education of natives. The living refutation of this claim by facts does not alter the petitioners' litany. The same chorus of voices is not at all silenced by the educational progress of the Bantu in the Republic. While visiting Turfloop University College in 1963, I could read western press reports about how South Africa parades sham schools before the eyes of visitors. Turfloop is not only a magnificently built collection of buildings, but its curriculum is exactly the same as in the rest of the Republic's university system, of which it is a part.* And it should be emphasized that Turfloop is only one of the several institutions of higher education for natives. It is ironic that one can point to some telling statistics which indicate that the percentage of children being educated in South West Africa is much

* This university comprises a collection of buildings with Venda folk *motives* in their architectural style. At night the central tower is illuminated so that these *motives* in beautiful colors are visible from afar, and evoke pride in the inhabitants of the area.

higher than in the rest of Africa, the chief petitioners, Liberia and Ethiopia included! Indeed, the percentage of school attendance by native children in South West Africa is exceeded only in Congo-Brazzaville, Kenya, and Nigeria, and chiefly in the Republic where it is 85%. It is expected that by 1970 this percentage will be 60% in South West Africa. Needless to add that scholarization is extremely low in Liberia and Ethiopia, the two accusers of South Africa, who offer gratuitous solutions to problems they are far from solving.

This is what an UNESCO publication on education (1961) writes about school enrollment in Africa: "Today for the African states as a whole, only 60% of school age children are enrolled. The situation varies from state to state, ranging from less than 2% in some to 60% in others. In the majority of cases, the proportion of children out of school exceeds 80%." For Liberia, the percentage in school is 23, Ethiopia 5!

What is the content of this education? Common sense and direct observation should be a good guide here. Anybody who has been to Turfloop or to the college of the Sons of Chiefs at Jongilizwe, or at the Augustineum near Windhoek, or has visited establishments as far apart in scope as kindergartens or the Radio Bantu in Johannesburg, knows that the South African efforts to educate the natives (and encourage their own efforts in this direction) are not only gigantic but sincere and honest. I cannot accept arguments that what happens in the Republic has no relevance to Pretoria's policy in South West Africa, because one of the petitioners' chief complaints is precisely that the government applies in the latter *all* the laws valid in the former. Having visited and studied both territories, I am in a position to assert that, indeed, the same policy is applied, originating from the same motives: the gradual lifting of the entire native population to the level of self-rule.

He who saw the achievements of white-encouraged Bantu efforts at Radio Bantu, can only say that western countries, priding themselves on their enlightened liberal policies ought to learn from the South Africans. It is certainly not the Indians in the United States who would be given a full-time radio program and the technical facilities to create and perform several-hours-long dramatic plays in their own languages, making use of the extraordinary resources of their native traditions and the incomparable talent of their artists. The supposedly racist South African regime, bent according to the petitioners and their white stooges on the physical and cultural destruction of the natives, sends these recordings abroad where they win, at best, third prizes because, as an Italian jury recently explained, South Africa is just not entitled to the first prize it deserves.

If such is the policy of the Radio Bantu, revival and strengthening of native culture, without in any sense neglecting the most modern interests, how could this same native culture be at the same time undermined and impeded at other levels? It is untrue that the natives are prevented from learning English and are obliged to study in their own languages which isolate them from the outside world. Whether in conversation with Mr. Mdedle, minister of education in the Transkei, or at the Augustineum at Windhoek, I could ascertain that lower grade instruction is given in the native language (as all pedagogical authorities say it should be), and Afrikaans and English are gradually introduced, particularly in scientific courses requiring it. That children should be educated in their mother tongue nobody except ferocious ideologues oppose, and then only when South African attitudes are debated. The argument that the native languages are backward is again untrue; as long as a language is spoken by a group of people, it grows and enriches itself, is shaped by the mentality of those who speak it, and in turn shapes his mentality.

On this point too the critics have not only shown bad faith, but also the most striking contradictions. At the conference of African States on the development of education in Africa held at Addis Ababa from the 15th to 25th of May, 1961, all African delegates concluded that the educational systems modeled on European countries "based as they are on a non-African background allow no room for the African child's intelligence, powers of observation, and creative imagination to develop freely, nor do they help him find his bearings in the world. For the African personality to assert itself, it is necessary to rediscover the African cultural heritage to which an important place should be alloted in education."

In spite of this commonsensical statement in the final report of the conference, in their charges against South Africa, Liberia and Ethiopia quote with approval an author whose thinking is exactly the contrary: "The whole myth of a separate native culture collapses when it is recognized that the African progress and emancipation depend upon an escape from the tribe and deeper entry into the life of the West. The indigenous nations of Africa have no culture of their own, or in any event, no culture worth preserving, not even as a foundation on which modern development can be based."

The reader will permit me a personal reminiscence from my years as a Hungarian youth in Rumania. The Hungarians formed between the two wars a minority of some three and a half million. From a practical viewpoint it would have been better for them, collectively and individually, to "abandon" their language (whatever that means and however it is done) and "adopt" Rumanian instead. This was the desire of the Rumanian authorities, who put all kinds of pressures on the minorities to dilute themselves as national entities. This would have also been the Hungarian language group's interest, because its language was a small isolated linguistic island in an ocean of German and Slav, whereas through Rumanian, they would have had access to the large stream of Romance languages. Yet at no time was such a move even envisaged; on the contrary, the Hungarian minority suffered repression, intimidation, and pressure rather than yield in its legitimate demands (guaranteed by the peace treaty at Trianon) for Hungarian schools, church services, newspapers.

Coming back to the Bantu in the Republic, and to the other native groups in South West Africa, it is obvious that their languages also form an essential part of their personality, culture and traditional existence.* It is equally true that they need Afrikaans and English and that these languages form the larger part of their curriculum in the higher grades. I noted a certain effort by the Afrikaners to push the Afrikaans language in the foreground of native education at the expense of English. This follows from the great national pride of the Afrikaner element, determined to pay back the British for their previous imposition of English and suppression of Afrikaans. But this has mere pinprick effects since after all, nobody can deny the importance of English. The overall result is that as in the Republic, in South West Africa too, the natives are becoming increasingly tri-lingual.

I mentioned earlier that in Mr. Löwenstein's description, courses offered to South West African natives, when offered at all, are limited to hygiene, handicraft, and religion. Let us note in passing the ideological angle of this remark: the author wishes to suggest that the South African white contract holders tie their workers to the kind of work by which white men too may profit, and to religion, evidently the "opium of the people" which makes them docile servants. Behind these remarks, there is, furthermore, a statement once made by Dr. Verwoerd that it is more important for the Bantu in their present circumstances to learn about planting an orchard than planning

* The permanent mandates commission of the League of Nations demanded that "in all mandated territories, smaller children should receive instruction solely in the native tongue." This is also the opinion of UNESCO pedagogues. "On educational grounds, we recommend that the use of the mother tongue be extended to as late a stage in education as possible." (Report on the Use of Vernacular Languages in Education, 1953.)

an atomic bomb. The statement may have been blunt, as so many others are that the South Africans make, but this does not take away its truth value. As I said about conditions of development in the new countries of Africa and Asia, it is more important that they feed their populations and provide them with the necessities than to engage in vast industrial projects which drain their material and human resources.

But the entire controversy about native education is pointless anyway, since the curriculum is not what the petitioners say it is. In addition to many classrooms I visited in South West Africa I spent some time at the Augustineum College at Okahandja near Windhoek. This school for non-whites was founded in 1866 on the bank of Swakop River and later moved to its present location. The day we arrived was the first of the students' return for the beginning of a new semester. Since classes were not yet in session I took the opportunity of looking into every nook and corner, talking with white and native teachers, and inspecting the dormitories.

The students, several hundreds of them, come from all parts of South West Africa, from the homelands as well as the Police Zone. Tuition, lodging, food, textbooks, and so on, are entirely free. Pocket money is provided for all when they go to town on Saturday afternoons. The Dormitories of the boys and girls (between the ages of fifteen and twenty, as I could guess, but some of them were older) consist of large, pleasant, simply furnished rooms, each for a group of ten. Although attempts have been made to allot the rooms without regard to tribal ties, the students always end by regrouping themselves according to tribe and language.

It was striking to see how well-behaved and disciplined they were as the various teachers read their names and organized the classes to be started the following day. When I remarked on their good behavior I don't mean that they were subdued, but that they had good manners, without which the work of educating them cannot be seriously pursued. The reader will appreciate, for example, the problem that the principal and the staff face: many of the youngsters arriving from the "backwoods" have never eaten at tables, never seen or used silverware. To teach them to keep the lovely refectory clean, the tables well set, and to eat as their city cousins do is a worthy task in itself, one which becomes inevitably part of the African education process.

I found in the principal, Mr. Du Plessis, the quintessence of the Afrikaner administrator. I hope he will not mind my description of him as characteristic of so many others of his colleagues in various posts. Mr. Du Plessis combines the qualities of matter-of-factness, thorough practicality and realism, and of monolithic devotion to a complex task. Only such men who entertain no doubt and have a missionary's faith can do the job of taking primitive and inert masses and fashioning them into individuals and efficient communities. Men like Mr. Du Plessis hardly exist any more in the western world, a world with a washed-away foundation; it is the foundation which is still intact in Southern Africa and which nourishes the Du Plessis's from its rich subterranean sources.

The Principal's every word cut into the very meat of reality so that I could not help comparing his explanations with the meaningless slogans that education officials in the United States, and increasingly in western Europe, pour into the collection of decaying ideas that our schools have become. Before departing for South West Africa I had attended in New York a typical huge university gathering where students are made to absorb cliches by their bored and boring academic elders. The main speaker of the three-day function was a high official of the Peace Corps, who wants to bring, no more, no less, "the world revolution to the American campus." How refreshing it was to listen, with the Peace Corps' demagogue's words still irritating my ears, to the Principal of the Augustineum! Mr. Du Plessis believes that the parents of these youngsters send them to school so that they may learn, acquire skills, become better men, and improve their chances in a society which demands more and more of the natives. Hence, he added, we cannot tolerate discipline problems; we punish bad behavior and negligent study. Whoever refuses to do his work gets out and someone else takes his place. On my question whether such things occur frequently and discipline is hard to enforce, the Principal offered a plausible explanation why such problems are infrequent. The African, he said, is used to discipline because the chiefs have always dealt severely, even with the smallest infractions.

The curriculum is the general one used in every school in South West Africa, and goes up to matriculation, the South African high school diploma, whose value however is said to be much higher than the one given in American high schools. It is comparable to the diploma given by European *Realschule* and *Ecole Secondaire.* The better students, that is those who earned the matriculation certificate may then go on to universities in the Republic (there are none yet anywhere in South West Africa) while students less endowed intellectually are oriented to artisan skills. We visited the carpentry and tailoring workshops on the school premises and admired the items that their graduates make: suits copied from the English magazines, desks and furniture usable in classrooms.

Some of the teachers whom I desired to meet were called away from their work of arranging their classes and reacquainting themselves with their students. I was understandably interested in what the liberal art teachers would say, since liberal arts courses are not taught to natives—according to South Africa's critics abroad. The charming and energetic lady who teaches English is also the mayoress of the town of Okahandja. Teaching English for her is not only the pleasure of communicating her language to eager students, but also the satisfaction of "showing the Afrikaners" how popular the English language is! A justified pride and a legitimate satisfaction!

This lady told us of her students' great application to overcome the disadvantage and disparity of background. This was consonant with what I had heard in a dozen other African countries: After all, pupils who never saw forks and knives and tablecloths cannot be expected to have even an inkling of the myriad objects that Shakespeare describes, let alone the notions with which he juggles. Foreign texts, our lady teacher explained, must be slowly digested, with frequent interruptions for ingenious explanations. This is true of simple texts as well as Shakespearean plays. But slowness is compensated for by long study periods: six hours of class a day, plus three hours for homework. This is a considerable dose by any standard and shows the thoroughness with which the South Africans pursue their task, so well characterized by Mr. Du Plessis when he said: "The government spends a lot of money on these youngsters. They must work hard to be worth the effort."

There is only one thing which baffles the English teacher, herself an elderly, but vivacious lady: the expressionless faces in front of her in the classroom, the lack of reaction and of humor. But this is only at the beginning of the semester; later on, she manages to establish rapport and then warmth begins to flow in her direction.

Another teacher was a young native, formerly the same lady's student. He teaches history and geography. Mr. Löwenstein with his bias says in his book that even when natives are allowed to study such subjects, they must learn under the guise of geography about their location and the roads crossing it, under that of history about the white man's victories over their own black ancestors. Let us once more correct this version of things: the students of Augustineum are learning about all the continents and also about their own history, as well as Roman, Greek, European and general African history. Incidentally, Mr. Löwenstein might have performed a more useful job if he had given time and concern to our own thinning Ameri-

can curriculum, with its solid subject matters disappearing, rather than to the supposed inadequacies of the
natives' intellectual training in South West Africa.

After having moved already once, seventy-five years
ago, the Augustineum is again changing locations. Just
outside Windhoek, on a hill dominating Katutura and the
Coloured township, we visited the six magnificent structures now nearing completion, and scheduled to house the
college. These buildings are several stories high and
modern in style. They are alloted to classrooms, labora-
tories, library, and dormitories for a total of six hundred
black students. Like its present location, it will continue
work in three directions, a two-year teacher-training institution, vocational education, and high school up to the
level of matriculation. It shows South African practical-
mindedness and planning ahead that the buildings are
expected to house the Augustineum only until the homelands themselves will have their own teacher-training
institutions. After that the buildings will be turned into an
educational institution for the Coloured in the vicinity.

What does the overall picture of native life in South
West Africa reveal? Slow and steady progress, to which
Pretoria is fully committed from a sense of practicality
and idealism, and from a thoroughly African vision. That
the ways and means of dealing with the problem are not
those of America and Europe cannot make them less valid
and valuable, but rather the contrary. The departing
European colonizers of other African countries left short-
range violence, and long-term cares behind them. It is
imperative that Pretoria should not imitate their example

and should not comply with their reckless advice. In the long run, the natives of South West Africa are likely to have a better future than the black men in other countries; the effect on them of Pretoria's policy, a policy which has good and bad elements, is that their moral fiber will be toughened, their indolence changed into initiative; in one word, that they will turn into pioneers of their own country.

PART TWO

The Case

CHAPTER 5

================================

CONFRONTATION

From the descriptions and analysis of Part One, the reader has obtained a general picture of the good and bad aspects of South West African life, the extraordinary complexity of its problems, hardly imaginable in our western world, where almost everything receives routine solutions and where computers are now ready to process the data of our external and internal existence. It is the shortcoming of books presenting a country that its paragraphs and sentences describe everything as *given,* as functioning with at least some ease. Reality as seen is always immeasurably more problematic: eye witnesses understand that what is, is the result of innumerable trials, errors, compromises, failures, successes. In other words, reality always appears as essentially fragile and precarious because it is sustained by the decisions of men. This precariousness is particularly apparent in a land like South West Africa where the incredible diversity of the population makes it difficult for the decisions of men to attain institutionalized, routine forms. When in addition to these difficulties we realize that South West Africa is today the object of a vicious international offensive, with not only this land's future involved, but also questions of law and precedent, then we can appreciate the effort to create here a viable society, progressing slowly out of its mainly unfavorable circumstances.

One example of the obstacles in the way of progress is that the recommendations of the Odendaal Commission are indefinitely blocked by the court case now proceeding at The Hague. Although the mandate given by the League of Nations to South Africa has to all intents and purposes lapsed, Pretoria is understandably unwilling to implement the proposed political structure for the home-land for the duration of the Case. This delay, by the way, is in the spirit of the mandate which made no provision whatsoever for a political structure of the territory. Naturally this is regrettable: The mandate was given forty-six years ago at a time when, as it was recognized, the natives were too undeveloped to have ideas of political organization in the western sense of the term. Meanwhile, however, they have obviously attained a higher degree of political maturity, although still far from the level required for a democratic system of voting. But since it is evident that South Africa is gradually preparing them for self-rule, why should the United Nations, supposedly concerned with South West Africa's future, impede the evolution—except for ideological reasons which have nothing to do with the merits of the case?

Instead of this logical course, the United Nations follows a different one: it encourages each and every individual and group, no matter how removed from South West African realities, to interfere with orderly development and create confusion and internecine war. Once again in the name of "peace" the United Nations instigates conflict and bloodshed, ready, however, to wash its hands and blame incidents on those who had warned against irresponsible words and actions.

The present political structure of South West Africa will form the topic of this chapter, so as to shed light on what is prepared by the underground, where its support originates, and what the role of the United Nations is in feeding its restlessness.

Professor Logan from Los Angeles told the Court in his testimony that he does not "believe there is anywhere in the world a more diverse population," than in South West Africa. This is evident to the traveler who saw the jungle populations of the Caprivi, the Bushmen of Okavango, the Coloureds of Rehoboth, the Germans of Luderitz and Swakopmund, the settled Ovambo, the unmixing Herero, and so on. To imagine that these ethnic groups might form a unitary state, elect officials side by side, intermingle their languages, cultures, and aspirations, is such an act of unrealism that only thousands of miles away are men irresponsible enough to indulge in it. Yet every statement by petitioners before the United Nations committees aims at proving that this idea is normal, natural and feasible. And they are not in the least inhibited by the successive explosions of so-called multi-racial states, on the same continent, even of states where mere tribal differences are strong enough to topple the whole edifice.

Although the "C" mandate had authorized South Africa to administer South West Africa through its own laws, in 1926 a law was passed granting South West Africa a constitution with a limited self-administration. A twelve-member legislative assembly was set up, elected by the white voters; the Administrator added to this number six other members appointed by him. A small cabinet of four chosen among the eighteen formed the executive organ assisting the Administrator. Since 1949, six of the South West African legislative assembly members have sat in the Parliament of the Republic of South Africa, and four in the Senate thus strengthening the links between the two territories.

This dual system raises the question of the white South Westers' national allegiance. They are inhabitants of the former mandated territory, and therefore technically not citizens of the Republic. But economic, political, and cultural ties make them look, when they scan the future, exclusively toward South Africa. For one thing, many of the some eighty thousand whites are South African citizens living in South West for business or other reasons. For another thing, the descendants of the territory's German inhabitants, as well as the new immigrants, are bound to see South Africa as their homeland, too. It is rather clear that the majority of the white population would not mind if the present situation, however unsettled in the eyes of international policymakers, remained indefinitely what it is. There is today among the whites such a thing as a

"South Wester personality," like the personality of the western states in the United States decades ago. For a typical South Wester, life in the Republic may appear as too soft and civilized, urbanized and sophisticated, whereas South West Africa is still a pioneer, even pre-pioneer country. Yet this feeling of being different does not mean at all that the South Wester whites, if given the alternative, would not choose annexation to the Republic, pure and simple, rather than a United Nations sponsored "multi-racial" state. Nobody wants to commit suicide, and the recent examples in Africa show conclusively that those whites who accept becoming minorities in a non-white-majority state (black or Arab) are cutting the branch on which they sit.*

It is fallacious to reason that the division of the South West African white electorate into voters for two antagon-istic political parties indicates their hesitation on this big overriding issue. People may be divided on any number of issues, they may even afford the luxury of not seeing the forest for the trees; the essential problem may be hidden for a long time by smaller interests. But it would be foolish to suppose that they do not understand what is at stake, particularly in a land where racial diversity is not yet hidden behind philosophical hairsplitting.

My talks with politicians, journalists, and private persons were most instructive in this respect. There are in South West Africa only two parties, the National Party,

* See in Chapter 7 the parallel which exists between Rhodesia at the present, and the hypothetical future of South West Africa under a United Nations sponsored solution.

which openly supports Dr. Verwoerd (and in fact coincides with the National Party of the Republic), and the United South West Africa Party, which without admitting it, is a replica of the United Party in Capetown's Parliament. Behind these two, it is not difficult to find the exact line-up that prevails in South Africa. The Nationalists are more or less monolithic, differing among themselves on relatively minor issues only. In view of the overall confrontation before which South West Africa now stands, I call "minor issues" the divergence of opinions on whether Pretoria (and the Windhoek administration) does not spend too much money beyond the financial capacity of both territories for native development. I know the case of a white engineer of a private company who left his job in disgust over what he called the growing discrepancy between ever harder living conditions for whites, and the "luxury projects" built for the blacks. I would not mention this, perhaps isolated, example of South Wester white dissatisfaction, if at the same time, a similar sentiment were not also making headway among the whites and National Party members in South Africa. In fact, this year's election in the Republic saw the emergence, insignificant as it may be, of a new Republican Party, whose platform calls for putting a stop to the expenses of the Bantustan project. However, these movements of opinion, even when articulated as the program of a party, have a natural limit, insofar as people know that there is no alternative to the government's Bantustan policy. This is even more clear to the whites of South West Africa whose comparative percentage is lower than that of the South

African whites, and whose black neighbors are far less evolved than the Bantu in the Republic. It is true that the National Party voter will always lament over the expenses involved, and over farms bought up by the government and turned over to the native homelands. But the reason why the party is getting more votes at each election is that the electorate knows: Investment in native development is investment in their own future security also.*

The divergence of views is far greater among the voters of the United Party. They form a minority, and even before the 1966 elections had only one representative in the Windhoek legislative assembly against seventeen for the Nationalists. As in the Republic, these people while voting for the party they traditionally voted for, entertain doubts as to the "morality" of their position. Hence, generally they remain disciplined voters for the party platform which is based on white rule over the whole of South Africa, but having voted, they prefer to close their eyes and, with a gesture of political schizophrenia, they privately adopt a more "progressive" view. This is easy, as it is without practical consequences, and meantime relieves the conscience of the burden of "racism." In the Republic, the effect of the schizophrenia was that some years ago a small Progressive Party seceded from the parental body, the United Party; in the South West things have not yet gone that far. But in the ideas of some opposition voters I

* The electorate of South Africa and South West Africa showed again at the elections of March 30, 1966, that in the immense majority it approves the National Party policies. The United Party has no members now in the Windhoek Legislative Assembly. The Nationalists have won all eighteen seats.

found the same thought processes as among voters of the Progressive Party in the Republic.

What is the stand of the opposition in South West Africa? I think an opposition newspaper editor, Mr. Engelbrecht, summed it up for me in the most cogent manner. Unwittingly he also helped me understand the mentality of the opposition as distinct from, but not contradictory to, their policy. It was a most instructive visit in his editorial office, and I listened to him fascinated, at so much unrealism in the face of South West Africa's situation in the world.

Upon hearing that I had traveled in the northern areas, Mr. Engelbrecht could not hide his triumph that he knew more about it without having seen it than I, an obviously innocent and misled foreigner. He took a picture from a drawer and as though calling my bluff, he put it down on the desk as proof of large-scale militarization of the area. I mentioned in an earlier chapter that I had to disappoint him: I had seen the air strip in question (at Ondangua); it and its like are essential in a rain-soaked zone where the soil is too soft for landing.* And since there are not enough good roads and the distances are too long, the only way to transport goods and people is by plane. I assured Mr. Engelbrecht that none of the strips I had

---

* As we were preparing to leave Runtu, we kept exchanging greetings with the kind of people who accompanied us to the "airport" (no asphalt strip, just a clearing covered with grass and pebbles). The pilot urged us to get on the plane, and after we did, the doors were immediately shut and we took off exceptionally fast. We learned later that the usual sudden rain had appeared at the other end of the clearing; had we stayed three more minutes, the rain would have reached us, making it impossible for the plane to take off from the softened ground.

seen, and there are far from enough of them, were adequate and long enough for landing jet planes, but only for medium-sized planes like Dakotas. But he remained adamant. In fact, he saw from my argument that I am hopelessly "biased."

His own bias was that the United Nations' charges against South Africa are infallibly correct. He insisted that the tarred road which now leads from Windhoek to the north is also part of the military plan, since he said that natives do not drive, they only possess bicycles! Since I could not believe that the grievances of the opposition are exhausted by these grotesque suggestions, I pressed Mr. Engelbrecht to tell me everything. The previous day I was told by another opposition journalist that the government "ought to hasten slowly instead of spending so much money on the natives who have no use for what is done and built for them." And he quoted some Ovambos who, back from the work period, declined to change their mode of living, preferred to continue drinking beer and having their wives work for them. But when I asked both of my interlocutors what they meant by "hasten slowly" and spending less money, neither could specify his point. I asked: "Do you mean the government ought not to have built the Ovambo irrigation canals and dams?" The two journalists, unknown to each other, reacted in the same way: by sneering at and belittling what the government is doing, and disbelieving its good faith. "Too much money is spent," Mr. Engelbrecht later repeated, "and besides, it does not cost Pretoria a penny. When it makes a loan to Windhoek, it charges interest for it."

I saw that another dead-end had been reached; the opposition had no alternative economic policy. Or, better put, minus the (theoretical) willingness to integrate the races, its program was not different from that of the government. How about the political platform? Here Mr. Engelbrecht was in his element. He outlined his party's four steps toward the multi-racial society that the United Nations favors, and that real life blows away each time it is put together. First step: each non-white group would be represented in the legislative assembly by a government-appointed white person; second step: the government would appoint white representatives approved by the respective non-white groups; third step: full representation for the Coloured; final step: native representatives elected by the natives themselves.

This is a beautiful plan and it has moreover a certain esthetic appeal on account of its symmetry. Maybe it was born over a chess board! But when I asked when would the fourth decisive step be taken, the answer was, as it always is, SOMETIME; not yet; later; it is to be seen; it depends. At any rate, Mr. Engelbrecht added, this program concurs with United Nations' intentions. This seemed to be the decisive test. And the United Nations, in which disagreements are "like within a family, that is peaceful," would not want to try any Congo-like operation in South West Africa. It merely wants an independent, peaceful South West Africa. This is exactly the platform of the Progressive Party in the Republic.

The much bigger question, unanswered, and probably unanswerable, is whether the natives would accept one or another policy. But first of all, do they have an articulate political will?

I believe that there are only approximations in this respect, white men guessing more or less intelligently or emotionally. Such simplistic answers to our questions as those given by the petitioners must be discounted because they are based on falsehood. The recordings that Mr. Löwenstein made in South West Africa of "interviews" are ridiculously inadequate for a considered judgment; he admits that the interpreters knew practically no English, and in one passage of his book, he writes that after half an hour's listening to several statements made in native languages, the "interpreter" finally yielded to his insistence and "translated"; "We say to U.N.O., help, help, help." Surely this is a great hit in some circles, but others may not consider it as evidence. It is less likely that Pretoria misjudges the direction of native desire for self-rule, since it is in the nature of things that nations, and the emerging ones are no exception, wish to be masters of their own destiny and reach that stage in harmony with their circumstances and their overall interests.

As far as I could ascertain, the South West African natives, used to town life, and working and living among whites, support apartheid policy. Having gauged white determination correctly, the great majority is realistic enough to take what is given, then wait and see. I consider this as healthy opportunism, the stuff of which political attitudes are usually made. Would the sophisticated ones among them prefer voting rights alongside with the whites? At first sight, this seems self-evident to us citizens of western countries. But under other climes, where the coexistence of races is an extremely delicate matter, and a twenty-four-hour-a-day problem, reactions are likely to be different. Mr. Tom Swartz, president of the Coloured Council in the Cape, a man of remarkable lucidity, told me: "True, the National Party has taken away our voting rights on the white electoral list, but did those rights benefits us in any sense? Between elections our interests were completely ignored. Every fifth year, United Party representatives used to visit us, pat us on the shoulder, only to forget their promises once the votes were delivered. The Nationalists play a more honest game; they don't want votes, they want separate development. But they do a great deal for non-white groups and put more money in our pockets than we ever dreamed of."

Mr. Swartz' view is not as rare as the reader might imagine. I talked with many black businessmen and leaders who insist on the need for their people to learn self-reliance and to stand on their own feet. They say, "Let us face it; no matter how fast and how far our people advance, they will perhaps forever remain second to the white; tolerated and patted on the shoulder, even helped, but nevertheless, only second." Some of these men have traveled in the United States. They say something like: "Your country will always remain racist, and the Negro will remain a kind of second-class citizen. All considered, their interests were better promoted in the South where a sort of apartheid existed; they became self-reliant. In the northern cities, with all the integration that Martin Luther King wants, they remain poor cousins."

The sober views of realists do not prevent agitators from moving among the masses. Their political credo is independence now, and their political sophistication is low. An opposition newspaper editor in Windhoek told me of a recent visit by a group of young men. In the course of the discussion they admitted that they want the white men to leave. Asked how the territory would then be administered, and the production level maintained, they said they would go to the bank for money. They smilingly refused to believe that banks do not just distribute funds, but are rather eager consumers of them too.

It would be vain to underestimate the role of these agitators. After all, they are instrumental in threatening and preventing the families in shantytowns to move to healthier townships, they form the gangs of intimidators in many instances. They resort to other tricks too; they sell party membership cards of radical organizations to unsuspecting Ovambos under the pretense that this will secure higher wages for them. This is how membership lists in parties to which the United Nations so eagerly listens are fattened up.*

What are these parties, how are they organized and financed? The concept of political parties is alien to the African natives as also are such concepts as "democracy," the "vote," and the various "ideologies" to which parties usually adhere. Communal problems among them have

---

* In spite of rumors to the contrary police are remarkably restrained in their dealings with agitators, although the latter very often provoke them (like at Sharpeville) in order to make a *cause célèbre* abroad. Instructions to police are strict and categorical, whether in dealing with riots or arrested men inside the jails. Any sergeant (and officers above him) not reporting acts of brutality within twenty-four hours is dismissed together with the policeman who committed the act.

usually been settled by traditional tribal authority. For example when Mr. Kaizer Matanzima, at present Chief Minister of the Transkei, faced the task of electioneering to get the votes and beat his rival, he showed himself reluctant to engage in this practice because, as chief, his authority needed nothing more to bolster it. In South West Africa, where Pretoria's Bantustan policy is less advanced than in the Republic, political party formation was not to be encouraged until parties might deal with the concrete problems of the homelands.

The idea of creating parties came thus from abroad, launched by South West African petitioners, living in New York. It was the already mentioned Mr. Getsen (also known as Mburumba Kerina) who initiated the formation of the first party. It was he who was author of a letter suggesting the appointment of various chiefs to high-sounding but empty positions in the "party." This unwitting tribute to the chiefs' authority and central role refutes, of course, the leftist theory that the chiefs represent no one, and that the people are behind the radical agitators.*

Since Mr. Getsen-Kerina formed the SWAPO (South West Africa People's Organization), some fourteen more parties have sprung into existence, some with only leadership but no members, others on ethnic lines. The latter are

* Incidentally, while officially belittling the chiefs' importance and publicly ignoring them, the British government (in its policy vis-à-vis Rhodesia), also recognized that nothing meaningful and durable can be done in Africa without the chiefs. Mr. Duncan Sandys, then head of Commonwealth affairs, told privately to the Rhodesian negotiators who were stressing the chiefs' political importance over against the people's contempt for nationalist agitators, that the smart thing to do would be to label the tribes "political parties" and the chiefs "party leaders." All of which justifies Pretoria's policy of cooperation with the chiefs.

fighting among themselves, and prove in advance, and in lieu of further demonstrations, the impossibility of a unified program and policy, let alone of a unified state. Besides Mr. Getsen does not even claim (in private, that is) that when he says "multi-racialism" he includes the whites. In a letter to an associate, he writes (in 1959), "Let the stupid Africans and Coloured agitators stop preaching multiracialism or partnership in South West Africa at the expense of the African people. We have had enough of this nonsense. Our position should be made clear to the whites. We want South West Africa back, no more, no less."* While this is still a "political" statement, even though highly irresponsible and virulent, others by the same author strike frankly a terroristic tone: they call for acts defying the government, for a refusal to move from the shantytown to Katutura, etc.**

The SWAPO has been organized by Ovambos abroad and claims to represent the Ovambo people. This is of course not true, because the Ovambo follow their traditional chiefs, who are known to have requested Pretoria to implement as soon as possible the Odendaal Commission's recommendations. But the "Ovambo," in the name of the party, was sufficient to trigger the formation of parties (abroad, and in reality having no other existence than that of United Nations lobbyists) by the Namas (SWAUNIO), the Bergdamaras (SWADU), the Hereros (Chiefs' Council), the Coloured (SWACO), and others. Attempts to

* From testimony at The Hague by Mr. Kurt Dahlmann.
** Any method is good for the purpose of getting the United Nations involved, and anybody is encouraged to petition in New York. Well known is the case of a nurse who reported "genocide perpetrated on black babies in South West African hospitals."

unite the various splinter groups into a united front
were made, because the Organization of African Unity,
headquarters at Addis Ababa, threatened that it would
not assist financially any party based on ethnic loyalties. These attempts at unity, however, have failed because no formation can be agreed upon by the leaders
of the various units. There is nothing surprising in this,
and similar infightings in other places have wrecked
Holden Roberto's movement, and a host of others. Mr.
Kapuuo, a Herero spokesman, admitted as much when he
said: "Tribalism and group loyalties are things which you
have to take into account in South West Africa for many
years to come."

If we think of the long history of national and other
clashes in Europe (to limit the comparison to that continent) and of the so far futile attempt to integrate and
unite, even to federate, these nations, we should not be
surprised to find South West African unity at less than the
planning stage. After all, in the Congo, in Nigeria, in the
Maghreb, or between Egypt and Syria, India and Pakistan, the unifying efforts have also failed or have remained inconclusive. The fact that the dream of unity is,
as the saying goes, "in the air," shows only that an abstraction hatched in the minds of ideologues is one thing,
and reality quite another.

For this and other reasons, the "political" parties I
mentioned have no roots in South West African soil, and
no tangible impact on the black population. The scene of
their activity is the United Nations, its lobbies and committees. These are fed with "information" from various

channels; the American Committee on Africa, the ultra-leftist Catholic Worker group, other more private and informal leftist organizations and individuals, and of course the petitioners of South West African origin. I know some of these groups and individuals, and I wonder if the reader can imagine the state of mind which is theirs, and the atmosphere in which they live. Both are impregnated with a kind of naive fanaticism and the conviction that they must only say the word and the world will conform to the one pattern they see as perfect. Since this perfection is rather distant they see reality as a series of scandals, as one permanent, intolerable insult to their own vision. What they can never comprehend is that their efforts to put reality on the Utopian inquisitors' rack causes much more woe, misery, and suffering than can ever be caused by the existing situation.

These few words may have created the impression that the individuals and organizations in question are led and staffed by innocents whose fanaticism is perfumed with good will. Unquestionably, there are such people among them. But there must be a lot of another kind also if we judge by the list of fantastic charges that they have brought over the years, and particularly by the ferocious calls for a crusade against South Africa, in which they see the last devilish obstacle to their vision of a peaceful multi-racial world.*

* This mentality is well illustrated in an article by Professor Dennis Cowan, who writes that since the ratio of whites to non-whites in South Africa is roughly the same as in the rest of the world, South Africa could, by setting the example of good race relations at home, persuade the world to put an end to racial frictions everywhere. This is a rather unsubtle way of burdening South Africa with the ills of humanity.

It is worthwhile to print here the list of accusations which read like a horror story, taken from some cheap magazine, specializing in the description of sadistic acts. Their impact on the unsuspecting reader is calculated the same way as Hitler used to calculate his enormous lies: the bigger the lie, the likelier that people will believe it, or at least some of it. After all, people are apt to reason, nobody would dare make such statements without grounds, nor make them before respectable international organizations. But the truth is that the accusations are without ground, but they are repeated often enough (another of Hitler's methods) to sound objective and irrefutable.

Petitioners testified that: South Africa was pursuing a policy of genocide and racial extermination in the territory;* the indigenous populations were herded into concentration camps, where they were treated like animals, and reduced to slavery; non-whites were deprived of their land, and confined to desert areas; the education system was designed to prepare non-whites for an inferior station in life; there was large-scale militarization of South West Africa, and missile and nuclear centers have been established.**

* One petitioner testified that the infant mortality rate among non-whites exceeded 99%.

** Outside Walvis Bay, which forms part of the Cape Province since British annexation in 1878, and where there is a military training camp of a battalion strength, there are no military installations in South West Africa. According to the provisions of the mandate South Africa must keep there "sufficient force to maintain law and order and protect the territory." This is done by a citizen force, one regiment strength (approximately 300 men) and by groups of citizens, organized in commandos on the Swiss model of territorial defense. These groups are recruited among local whites (under South African laws, non-whites are not called to the

Added to these is a generous dose of other atrocities mentioned: police horsewhipping natives and driving them to work; natives anxiously watching each time a white man reaches into his pocket, that he might pull a revolver on them; whites in constant readiness to slaughter large numbers of natives; and so on.

One does not know by what one should be more amused: the petitioners' malevolent inventiveness or the credulity of the United Nations Fourth Committee. At any rate one would imagine that having such excellent trump cards in their hands, and having also the full attention of the United Nations, the petitioners and the Applicants (Liberia and Ethiopia) at the World Court would make full use of these advantages. One expected that they would triumphantly bury South Africa under an avalanche of proofs, substantiated by a daring parade of witnesses. One expected that the voluminous dossier presented by the South African legal team would be answered by Mr. Gross and his clients, point by point, showing the inexactitudes, the exaggerations, the lies, the malevolence, *in fine* the criminal vainly claiming innocence.

Instead of this . . .

---

colors) and there are no South African soldiers doing military service anywhere in the territory, although the mandate would authorize it. To speak as the petitioners do of missile-tracking stations and nuclear centers established secretly in South West Africa only proves their irresponsibility as well as those who arrogantly claim to speak as "delegates of mankind."

U.S. General S. L. A. Marshall, testifying before the World Court, declared that not only are there no military installations in South West Africa, but that it is the world's most underequipped part, from the point of view of military preparations.

CHAPTER 6

FACTS AND FABRICATIONS

. . . INSTEAD OF THIS, Mr. Ernest Gross announced at the hearing of May 19, 1965 that: "the Applicants [Liberia, Ethiopia] have advised the Respondent [South Africa] as well as this honorable Court that all and any averments of fact in Respondent's written pleadings will be and are accepted as true, unless specifically denied. And Applicants have not found it necessary, and do not find it necessary, to controvert any such averment of fact. Hence, for the purposes of these proceedings, such averments of fact, although made by Respondent in a copious and unusually voluminous record, may be treated as if incorporated by reference into the Applicants' pleadings."

In less formal, plain language, this meant that with a truly dramatic *volte-face*, Mr. Gross's clients threw out all their own previous and voluminous allegations, disavowed all the witnesses and petitioners of the past decade, and accepted as true the South African version of the mandate territory's situation. The question is why did the two accuser countries and behind them the committees appointed by the United Nations and those whom Mr. Gross, in the original submission of the case had described as "a variety of independent sources," admit more than tacitly that Pretoria had been right all along? The Applicants' charges run to many thousands of words, and the dossiers of the United Nations regarding South West Africa are far bigger still. Yet, Mr. Gross's statement is an absolutely clear admission that their pleading contains such substantial untruths that the Court where the atmosphere is not so fanatical as at the United Nations, could not be expected to believe them. I mentioned before that when South Africa offered to pay the expense of bringing the Applicants' witnesses to The Hague, they rejected the offer. I also mentioned that the Applicants vehemently argued against a visit by the Court to the premises, a visit which could have been conclusive.

Common sense can only offer one explanation for this behavior: the Applicants did not trust the veracity of the very same witnesses ("independent sources"), on whose testimony over the years they had built their whole case! They in fact were so dubious of the allegations concerning the true situation of South West Africa that they opposed the idea of a Court visit, which would have exposed the shabby nature of the witnesses' concoction.

All this was like the behavior of children or of completely irresponsible people. At any rate, it was a gigantic loss of face. And the impression was not improved by the statement of the Liberian delegate at the Trusteeship Committee, after the about-turn at The Hague: "The fact of the matter is," said Miss A. Brooks, "that Liberia and Ethiopia are relying on the legal aspect of the case. It is for that reason that we have not brought numerous witnesses before the Court as South Africa has done."

These were the statements on and shortly after May 19th. Now we must look behind the statements in order to unravel the whole mechanism of fabrication. After all, even leaving aside for the moment the merits of the concrete case, whether or not South Africa misadministers the South West and destroys its non-white population, it remains still that an impudent slap was administered to the World Court on May 19; an act of contempt was committed toward a highly respected international judicial body. At one time, the president of the Court, Sir Percy Spender, of Australia, felt compelled to snap at lawyer Gross: "What is then, the exact nature of your pleading?" He asked with understandable impatience. As the chief representative of the South African legal team put it: "The Applicants expect the Court to formulate their case for them."

There is then, in the first place, the use of the Court for demagogic purposes. It is not an exceptional behavior. Similar acts of contempt for elementary rules of international conduct have been committed by certain nations which, by their indecent language, and verbal violence, are literally browbeating the moderate ones into supporting resolutions contrary to accepted standards. Some of such resolutions have demanded the exclusion of Portugal, South Africa, etc., from international bodies of a non-political character to which they rightfully belong as dues-paying and constructive members. Mr. Gross and his clients had introduced, then, irresponsible and illegal attitudes to the very institution which is supposed to embody the search for civilized relationships among nations.

But there is more than that. The entire case from which the arrogant conduct of Mr. Gross's clients cannot be separated must be viewed as a phase in the conflict between the rule of law observed by civilized sovereign nations in their mutual policies and the ideology-inspired behavior in the United Nations. The United Nations, increasingly from its early beginnings, has been the exponent of the kind of starry-eyed optimism about individuals and nations which, when thwarted as it must be, turns into its opposite, a vicious will to destroy whatever does not conform to its blueprints. But even without the theoretical aspect, it is obvious that there are, within the United Nations, groups of nations which seek domination, first of this body, then, by increasing the latter's power beyond all measure and restraint, of all global arrangements. This drive is, needless to say, the old *libido dominandi*, enlarged to include the whole earth. Like all such previous attempts, it is advertised as bringing peace, security, and happiness to all.

The whole history of the "South West Africa case" is a clear demonstration of this will to rule. Thus, it is important that the mechanism of the case, and the history of the applicants' pleading should be exposed, lest future instances might be won by the United Nations, simply by resting on the precedent. For the South West Africa case contains all the elements that may reappear in future cases: false statements, the technique of the big lie, internationally endorsed; a well-orchestrated press campaign to influence world opinion; and finally a court case presented in such a way as to overwhelm a defendant whom one tried to demoralize beforehand. These well-coordinated actions are interspersed among dramatic hearings at the UN and by visits by United Nations inspection teams resulting in false reports.*

Thus, the stage is set for any number of new performances. The lawlessness and ideological fanaticism of all this is quite clear, although it is evident that at each step, a majority of well-intentioned members, favoring objective procedures, must be sidestepped, browbeaten, or coerced by the demagogic minority into accepting a disreputable course of action. One may sympathize with such a majority, whether individuals or groups; but it is necessary to find safeguards against the irresponsible minority, and particularly against an institution with claims of universality when it allows itself to be dominated by fanatics and their dishonest methods. The world in which we live, this, alas, defective, sublunar world, has always known plenty of troubles from the unruly, the self-seeking, the fanatic, although in the past, these have wielded partial power only; if in the future, we allow an international agency to accumulate all power, through yielding to its demands in such test cases as the South

* It is noteworthy that while Applicants opposed the visit of South West Africa by members of the Court, they eagerly urged such a visit by a United Nations commission in 1962. Would it be that they trusted the latter to come up, regardless of the actual findings, with a favorable report, whereas they knew they could not influence the former?

West Africa case, then we should be prepared for a world dictatorship to rule over us, a world dictatorship worse than Hitler's and Stalin's, because by definition no refuge could be found from its long arms.

The South West Africa case, in its present form, began on November 4, 1960, with the filing of charges at The Hague, against South Africa. It is necessary, for a full understanding of the developments since then, to give here a brief summary of the United Nations' campaign against South Africa, during the previous decade. The summary will show that not the petitioners, as such, nor even Liberia or Ethiopia are responsible for the relentless pressure, falsehoods, and aggressive intent, but that these methods have been devised by various United Nations committees and approved by the General Assembly. Nothing new was added to the charges by the Applicants at The Hague; they were a mere irresponsible mouthpiece for a group of nations for whom the United Nations has provided an atmosphere of demagogy and wild projects.

In 1946, Marshal Smuts proposed to the United Nations that South West Africa might be incorporated into the Union. This step had been preceded by a South West Africa-wide referendum in which all chiefs speaking for their respective tribes expressed their approval, with the exception of the Hereros, who refused to cooperate with the government. As the United Nations was also inclined to oppose the step, although it merely "took note" of South Africa's intention, the latter decided not to insist. In fact a year later, Pretoria submitted a report to the United Nations on its administration of the territory, an act of courtesy, which, however, did not amount to recognition of the Trusteeship Committee's authority.

There followed between 1950 and 1962 various attempts to settle the problem. Even partition of the territory was at one time suggested. In general, moderate resolutions were drafted until, toward the end of the 1950's, there developed a majority in the General Assembly referred to as the Afro-Asian bloc. Assisted eagerly by the Communist countries, members of this bloc began to fill the Committee on South West Africa, year after year; not only was clear preference given henceforward to South West African petitioners and their wild tales, but these tales were incorporated, without any critical evaluation, into the draft resolutions presented by the committee to the General Assembly. In their new policy to please the Afro-Asian bloc and not to antagonize it, the western powers too began to switch their votes from the earlier supported moderate drafts to the aggressive ones. Thus, the General Assembly accepted at its face value the drafts coming out of the South West Africa Committee, and the latter, also uncritically, accepted the version given by the petitioners. This seems like a naive method; but if we look at the nations whose delegates usually served on the South West Africa Committee, we realize that not naivete but politics of a certain kind was involved. Except for the Philippines and some Latin American delegates, the countries which were to pass judgment on South Africa and its administration were such stalwarts of democracy and human rights as Communist Hungary, and pro-communist Guinea and Ghana.

On November 4, 1960, Liberia and Ethiopia instituted proceedings against South Africa at the World Court. Two years later (December 21, 1962) the Court, answering South Africa's contention that it has no jurisdiction over the matter, decided by an extremely close vote, eight to seven, that it does have such a jurisdiction, and invited the litigants to present their respective pleadings. Yet, while the case was referred to the Court, and both parties were to abstain from further pursuing it according to the *sub judice* principle, the Committee on South West Africa voted to send a fact-finding commission to the territory.

Thus took place in 1962 one of those shady episodes which mark the United Nations' history: uncalled-for interference, irresponsible remarks by its highest officials, whether Dag Hammarskjold or U Thant, and the shameless use of double standards. The story, which reads like a comic opera, deserves to be told in some detail.

The Committee on South West Africa, after securing Pretoria's invitation, delegated its chairman, Mr. Carpio of the Philippines, and its vice-chairman, Mr. DeAlva of Mexico, to make a visit to the contested territory, accompanied by a suitable staff. Pretoria drew up an itinerary, making it clear, however, that the short time, ten days, that Mr. Carpio and Mr. DeAlva intended to spend in South West Africa, was far from sufficient. The gentlemen of the United Nations were told that should they desire to extend the period of their visit, and include other places in their itinerary, the South African government would give instructions accordingly to the local authorities. Mr. Carpio was, however, in a hurry to take up his new duties as ambassador of his country to Egypt and declared himself satisfied with the arrangements and the duration of the trip. In fact, he shortened it by two days, and even refused to travel to some places, sending his vice-chairman instead.

On their return to Pretoria, the two travelers held a number of meetings with Dr. Verwoerd and members of his government. But Mr. Carpio attended only one such meeting, after which he fell ill and for the rest of the time, he was either hospitalized or confined to his sick bed in his hotel. He gave full authority meanwhile to Mr. De-Alva to continue the talks with the South African government; the two men were to consult at Mr. Carpio's bedside after each such meeting.

The South African government asked to be told of the results of their observation tour, since for years the charges had been wildly brandished about militarization, police brutality, and genocide in South West Africa. Mr. DeAlva immediately admitted that he had seen no signs of any; Mr. Carpio first began by hedging, saying that after all he could only make such "statements concerning places they had visited, but not others." Whereupon the Prime Minister suggested that a military plane would be at once put at their disposal or at the disposal of any two military attaches accredited to Pretoria whom they may designate to fly to the places not yet visited (fifteen such "military bases" were on Carpio's list, although he mentioned only four) and check the truth or falseness of the charges. Mr. Carpio declined the offer and when the sessions resumed he accepted that there was no evidence of militarization.*

At other sessions, the visitors also admitted that they had found no evidence of any threat to international peace and security within South West Africa; of the indigenous population being exterminated;** of political prisoners being detained.

The South African government was obviously pleased to hear that the United Nations fact-finding missions' conclusions amounted to a complete refutation of the charges contained in the petitioners' statements. The two parties proceeded then to issue a joint communiqué as it had been previously agreed.

At this point begins the second act of the comedy. While Mr. DeAlva was acting according to the code of honor of diplomats and gentlemen of the happier, pre-United Nations days, Mr. Carpio became obviously concerned over his reputation as a dutiful Afro-Asian rah-rah man. After all, he was to take up ambassadorial duties in

* This ought to have refuted conclusively allegations contained in the report of the Committee on South West Africa of the year before (1961): "The Committee draws attention to the fact that the mandatory power has encouraged the arming of the European population of the territory, and has established military fortifications and large defense forces within the mandated territory, and has at the same time revised the integrated military program of the territory and South Africa to provide, among other things, for a citizen force of wartime strength and a speedup of the production of arms and munitions." Needless to say, that said Committee, ignoring the admission of its lies by its own two delegates, continues to maintain the above allegations. It has only brought them "up to date" by adding that missile stations and nuclear centers are also among the military installations in South West Africa.

** At the beginning of the mandate in 1921, there was in South West Africa a non-white population of 190,000; forty years later, the figure was 467,000 (non-white).

the capital of a chief Afro-Asian demagogue, Nasser; besides, how was he to face his colleagues, the Hungarians and the Guineans, of the South West Africa committee back in New York, if, instead of triumphantly returning, with damning dossiers, he put his name to a document exonerating the South Africans? The reader should be reassured; I am not trying to read Mr. Carpio's mind as he was lying in his hotel bed; I am merely paraphrasing the record by Carpio's colleague, Mr. De-Alva, who had to run errands between a reluctant Carpio and the patiently waiting South Africans. Finally, in the presence of their staff, Mr. Carpio agreed to a communiqué whose salient points are given above; the vice-chairman was then able to put an end to the shabby game.

Or so he thought. Mr. Carpio had reserved the last weapon and made use of it on his return to New York. The weapon was a trusted and age-old one: he denied everything; that he had signed a communiqué, that he had agreed with its text; that he had admitted not finding evidence according to the United Nations charges, and so on. For good measure, he went further: he claimed that he had been poisoned while in South West Africa, then nearly killed in the Pretoria hospital. After which he affixed his signature to the previously quoted Report of the Special Committee for South West Africa. The reading of this report, whose allegations are of course in direct contradiction with the joint communiqué published by the two parties in Pretoria, provides special entertainment through the addition of annexes. These annexes contain the various letters in which Mr. Carpio backtracks from

the communiqué in all-too-transparent efforts at self-justi-
fication, while Mr. DeAlva describes his colleague's conduct and all but calls him a liar. A recommended reading
to all those who still have illusions about the United
Nations as a pinnacle of humanity's hope and honor!

Needless to say, the South West Africa Committee of
the United Nations chose to accept the "findings" of Mr.
Carpio, and not the conclusions of the communiqué. In
other words, no attempt was made at balancing the petitioners' fantastic stories with the evidence as seen by the
very mission that the committee had delegated to investi-
gate things on the spot. In yet other words, the United
Nations is not interested in the truth arrived at by a
judicious weighing of statements from both sides; its
verdict, arrived at with the arbitrariness of the Star Cham-
ber, is reached long before the defendant presents his
case, and no amount of facts is able to sway these judges.
As if the accumulated demagogy had not been enough, in
1963, a new committee on "colonialism" was formed by
the United Nations, whose task it now became to keep
harassing Pretoria in lieu of the somewhat exhausted
South West Africa Committee. It is a sure indication of
the continuing decay of the United Nations that, while
its one-time General Secretary, Dag Hammarskjold, had
seen it fit to travel to South Africa and confer with its
statesmen, his successor, U Thant has not accepted Pretoria's invitation to see the situation for himself. Instead,
he, the supposedly supranational, thus impartial, "world
official," lashes out against South Africa, and ignoring also
the *sub judice* principle, commands it from the height of

all the thirty-eight floors whence he contemplates the world, to obey the United Nations resolutions.

* * *

Let us now switch back to the courtroom in The Hague, where Mr. Gross made the astounding statement (May 19, 1965) that his clients are not prepared to contest any statements made by the South Africans in the course of their presentation of evidence. Since this presentation, the most voluminous in the history of the Court, amounts to some one million words, and covers in minute detail all aspects of South West Africa, and all the allegations by the petitioners, Mr. Gross's declaration really means that not one word of his clients' charges, the charges solemnly reiterated by the United Nations and its committees, was true or could be substantiated. As we have seen, Miss A. Brooks, the Liberian delegate at the trusteeship committee, asserted immediately afterwards that the Applicants were anyway relying only on the "legal aspect" of the case. One wonders why? The Court had decided in December, 1962, that contrary to South Africa's contention, it did possess the competence to adjudicate the matter. Thus Liberia and Ethiopia had nothing to fear; their case in its purely formal aspects was considered a valid one by an obviously seriously deliberating court.

It is much more likely that Mr. Gross had never relied on the petitioners' testimony, was therefore apprehensive of a Court visit to South West Africa, and had from the beginning decided to shift his pleading if and when the situation becomes too uncomfortable for his clients. For example, when asked by one of the judges at the beginning of the hearing, whether he will call witnesses of his own, Mr. Gross declared that, "it was irrelevant to call witnesses *as it will be clear in the further proceedings.*" (Italics added.)

It is thus clear that the dramatic shift had been foreseen and prepared as a last recourse if it becomes obvious that the Court, unlike the United Nations, cannot be fanaticized, nor asked to act as a rubber stamp for the views of majorities in political bodies. In what did the shift consist?

Since now the Applicants' original charge fell by the wayside, namely that South Africa violated Article 2, Paragraph 2 of the mandate, according to which it was required "To promote to the utmost the population's material and moral well-being, and social progress," new batteries had to be brought urgently from the rear to the forefront. In the name of his clients, Mr. Gross now contended that from the twenty years' labor at the United Nations and other international organizations, a "norm or standard" had been born which forbids discrimination in any form whatsoever against, and even for, any part of the population. He alleged that these "norms of non-discrimination and non-separation" had been established by a kind of international consensus, expressed mostly at the United Nations, and that this represents the collective judgment of the collective will of the organs of the international community.

This is as exactly as possible the international application of J. J. Rousseau's theory of the General Will, a theory from which all modern totalitarian regimes logically and historically originate. For the main characteristic of the General Will is that it is not the sum total of the citizens partial wills, but a will impossible to localize and ascertain, but nevertheless binding. Even if nobody wills it, even if it seems contrary to the express desire of the citizens, the General Will is still valid and its adoption imperative. Thus, a minority party or group, sufficiently convinced of its own program, and lacking scruples, can simply assert that it and it alone represents the General Will, the "dormant" or "unexplicited" will of all the citizenry. Such a totalitarian party can then impose its ideology and methods, and can proceed with the "persuasion" of the terrorized population that its program is the highway to happiness.

This is the pernicious contention of Mr. Gross for his clients too. Through his mouth, the Applicants assert that the Court cannot express a view as to what does or does not promote well-being and progress; all that the Court can do is to give effect to the "norms and standards, the judgments and the condemnations" already elaborated by the organized international community. If accepted, these doctrines would first of all paralyze the work of the Court, which would be called upon to accept as pre-existing and binding law the verbal fancies indulged in by various demagogues at the United Nations, who of course hardly practice what they preach anyway. In the second place, the doctrine was made to measure for the Applicants, because with its help, they forestall any factual investigation of South West Africa by the Court.* For indeed: They do not now contend that the South Africans' discrimination vis-a-vis that non-white population (apartheid) has ill effects, or that it flows from ill motives; it merely states that differentiation among various parts of the population is wrong *per se,* according to the corpus of international decisions. As the Applicants put it, "Differential allotment would be illegal, even if it were intended for the benefit of the inhabitants of the territory."

The one beneficial effect of this twisted pleading was that it simplified matters considerably. Indeed the issue to decide now was whether there is in actual fact such a "norm or standard." And: Can the various international bodies, which are battlegrounds of partial interest, and *not* supranational expressions of humanity's interests, create norms? And: Is it enough to make high-sounding speeches about an ideal norm, and even approve it by majority vote, without actually practicing it? Can anybody claim that the norm as defined by Mr. Gross is in actual practice?

If it is not, then let us all take Justicia's scale in our hands and proceed with the detection and chastisement of the guilty parties, not merely of South Africa. But this is where a great surprise is awaiting us! For it turns out that in Professor Stefan Possony's words before the World Court, there are no fewer than *fifty* countries where the law allots rights, duties, and burdens on the basis of membership in a group, class or race! And *forty* out of

* The switch had been made naturally before the Court decided not to visit South West Africa or any other African territory.

these 50 countries are members of the United Nations! !
And they include, lo and behold, the Applicants, Liberia
and Ethiopia! What kind of a norm is this for which half
of the United Nations' membership shows such a scorn as
to legalize its opposite?

It would be tedious to enumerate here all the fifty
instances, plus a few more, because not even the expert in
international affairs can gauge all the varieties of social
experience. But: The study of what man does to man is,
whether good or bad, so fascinating that it might be
worth our while to list some examples. The reader, accustomed to his daily fare of international platitudes on the
pages of newspapers, may actually be led to believe that
mankind is approaching the new Jerusalem of uniformly
kind behavior toward his neighbors. He may be led to see
everywhere an emerging norm of generosity, or at least a
frictionless state, an aseptic atmosphere, which encourages conformist behavior.

Such a picture is absolutely false, notwithstanding the
pious slogans promoting it. Even such an abstract document as the Declaration on Racial Discrimination adopted
by the United Nations in 1963 must take cognizance of
the general and indestructible human reality. After con-
demning the theory that mankind is divided into races,
and after calling on all states not to practice discrimination on the basis of race, color, or ethnic origin, Article 2
of the Declaration goes on, saying: "Certain concrete
measures might be taken in appropriate circumstances in
order to secure the adequate development or protection of
individuals belonging to certain racial groups."

We may perhaps suspend judgment on whether the instances below are in or against the spirit of Article 2. Whatever we think about their reasonableness, they are undeniable facts expressed through laws.

1) The Republic of Liberia is divided, according to law, in two sections: a coastal strip of about forty miles wide, and the interior of the country. In the first, only the evolués (black) can live and own property, and the judicial system is based on Anglo-American law. In the second, the tribal system prevails, and each tribe has its own organization. It is among the tribes that the coastal entrepreneurs recruit their manpower, after signing work contracts, not with the individual workers, but with the tribal chiefs, who of course put some profit into their own pockets, too. Families of the workers are not supposed to accompany them to their place of work in the coastal zone. The reader might profitably compare this system with the one in Ovamboland, and wonder, incidentally, about apartheid being the policy of a black country vis-à-vis its black but not evolué population.*

2) The Housa-speaking Moslem northerners (black) of Nigeria despise the Christianized black tribesmen, their fellow citizens. Formerly, the Moslems kept slaves caught among the non-Moslem tribes and traded them in the slave markets of Kano, Sokoto, Zaria, and Maiduguri. Slavery has been abolished, but the northerners still keep the tribesmen at a distance, and segregate them into settlements called *sabongaris,* outside their cities' walls.

* The Liberian constitution makes it clear that "non-blacks may not accede to Liberian citizenship."

3) In India, Pakistan, Ceylon, and Burma (Secretary General U Thant's country), five hundred million people live divided according to the complex system of eight hundred and four castes. And the "untouchables" remain untouched.

4) Multiconfessional Lebanon also has a complicated system of allotment of parliamentary seats, in order to prevent endless frictions among the religious communities. Five-elevenths of the seats are reserved for the Moslems, six-elevenths for Christians. The town of Tripoli, for example, has five representatives, of whom four must belong to the Moslem Sunnite sect, one to the Greek Orthodox faith.

5) Strict linguistic discrimination exists in Belgium, separating the country into a Flemish and a Walloon zone, along very complicated and always contested lines.

6) In Syria, Moslems and non-Moslems do not share the same rights. Before the courts, the Moslem's testimony has a greater weight than that of a non-Moslem. A non-Moslem may not inherit from a Moslem, but the latter may inherit from a non-Moslem.

7) The constitution of Cyprus, approved by the United Nations, stipulates that all citizens must belong either to the Greek or to the Turkish community. Seventy percent of all parliamentary representatives must be Greek, and also the president of the Republic. The vice-presidency and thirty percent of the seats in the parliament are alloted to the Turks.

Many other examples could be given; but we don't have to go fetch them from other parts of the globe, we find them right here at home. In vain does the American people choose to live in the future; the past accompanies us forever, and ought to teach us some modesty. White men in the United States have had to deal with two different-colored, racially different groups: the Indians and the Negroes. The former were both numerically weak and unusable, unbreakable, undomesticable in farm and factory. Consequently, we destroyed them, often in ways that might make the South Africans shudder. Those who escaped destruction we have confined in reserves, where many of them live in justified hatred of the white man, and have degenerated to the lowest possible level of indignity; they are used now as tourist attractions in Arizona, Colorado, and New Mexico.

The second group, numerically stronger, having mixed their blood with the whites, and usable for work, we did not exterminate. We have shut them up in visible (Harlem) and invisible reserves, treated them as third-class citizens, good to fight in wars, but not to sit down with at the same table.

Such a record is anything but proud. Yet the reader might argue that the darkness of it is now disappearing. I have my doubts about that, but this is not the point. Even if it is a thing of the past, which it is not, it is indecent and repulsive, to say the least, to begin assuming the moralizer's role, and shout abuse at others who are not worse than ourselves, although they have an immeasurably bigger problem to contend with. I shall never forget a blindingly clear example of American hypocrisy in dealing with South Africa. A round table was called together in 1964 in Washington by a self-styled "peace promoting" organization, which shall remain charitably unnamed. The announced objective was to invite various people knowledgeable on Africa, and some South Africans as well, and discuss ways and means to "help" South Africa get out of its "tragic situation." The hypocrisy of the whole affair was in itself sickening; but the scandal cried to heaven, since we gathered at the Cosmos Club where no black man was admitted to enter! And we, the presumptuously debating white men, were served at the ensuing dinner by Negro waiters, the only ones of their race allowed to enter such exclusive premises.

CHAPTER 7

▪▪

PROSPECTS FOR SOUTH WEST AFRICA

I HOPE to have given in Part One as complete a description of South West Africa as possible in the framework of a brief study, with a two-fold purpose: the first was to acquaint the reader with a fantastic and interesting land, one of the last in the world about which very little is known, a true pioneer country. I wanted also to show, inadequately as one can do through the abstract screen of words, that this land has similarities to what parts of the United States must have looked like to its nineteenth-century immigrants and pioneers. My second purpose was to show South West Africa being used as a political football, like many other unfortunate countries of Africa and Asia today. It is essential for the reader to understand that South West Africa is not just a "controversial" corner of today's international politics, but that it constitutes a test case beween two contending concepts. One is the concept of national sovereignty, with all its weaknesses, defects, but also practical advantages; the other is the ideology of world dictatorship and global power in the disguise of "humanity's interests."

With only the first point in mind, I would have written a travel book of South West Africa; but the second point is urgent since, if the forces of demagogy and destruction, embodied by certain countries, and not resisted by others, have their way, the South West Africa case will serve as a precedent for irresponsible, but well-planned, intervention in anybody's affairs whose policies are disliked by the new international pirates. And then the world, under the façade of unity and brotherhood, will have been divided in two unequal parts: the minority, with constructive even though imperfect policies, and the majority, caring not for reasonable solutions, for complex human problems, but bent only on securing power for despots and bureaucrats.

Among the examples of United Nations intervention with just this result we may mention the case of the ex-Dutch western half of New Guinea. Under Dutch occupation, the Papuan Islanders, one of the world's most primitive groups, were slowly advancing out of their stone age existence. Then one of the mischief-makers of our times, Sukarno of Indonesia, laid claim on them, on the flimsy ground that having taken over all Dutch possessions in the area, he has a right on Western New Guinea too. Neither ethnically nor by historic rights could the Papuans "belong" to Indonesia; but the power game being what it is, Sukarno's demands were met by setting into motion the whole hypocritical method of so-called United Nations mediation. The territory was turned over to the United Nations (after the Dutch evacuated it), which acted as a fence for international highway robbers: saving the Dutch's face, it is not The Hague negotiators but the United Nations which hands over "West Irian" to Sukarno. This organization, eager transactor of the world's shady deals, is of course strengthened by each new dubious role thrust into its hands. The future of New Guinea seems thus settled, although the world press chooses not to mention the Papuans' sorry plight. We hear not a word of Papuan refugees from Sukarno's soldiers, trying to cross over to the Australian half of the island.

But the future of South West Africa is still open, at least officially. We shall devote this last chapter to the examination of what this future may hold.

The international abstraction-makers with their love of figures sincerely believe that majorities must everywhere rule. There are some eighty thousand white men in South West Africa, and half a million blacks. The equation shows that the latter must rule, with or without the former's consent or presence. But there are other equations, too, hard to express in figures, yet closer to life. It seems that wherever white men settled in the temperate zones of Africa (near the peaks or on high plateaus) they became permanent inhabitants—not a settler or a *colon*. They organized their environment, made the soil fertile, and the economy productive. Equally important: they provided opportunities for their black neighbors, and even for faraway black men to increase, multiply, and prosper. In short, they refuse to leave where the abstraction makers try to throw them out like undeserving servants.

It seems then that there is a number below which the

white community can be compelled to pack and get out, above which it digs in and nothing short of war can dislodge it. (The question is not just of numbers, but primarily of will, organization, and the capacity to create a distinct civilization out of a wild environment.) Only one such situation existed in Africa north of the Equator, Algeria. The others are all in southern Africa.

The Algerian white men (one million, two hundred thousand of a total population of ten million) finally yielded, packed and got out, not because some Marxist-invented "wind of history" was blowing, but because 1) they were demoralized by contradictory policies; 2) they were too close to France whence special troops could come over and crush their resistance; and 3) they were French citizens, knowing in the back of their minds that at the end of their Calvary they could still return to their mother country. These three factors and nothing else broke their morale after which the "clean-up operations" were easily successful.

But the situation is entirely different in southern Africa, whether in Rhodesia or in South West Africa. In fact, the two have certain similarities. The uncertainty of Rhodesians with regard to British policy, and the increasingly apparent duplicity of Harold Wilson's government in its "negotiations" with Salisbury, finally determined them to proclaim independence: the alternative was to be sacrificed to London's hope against hope to salvage a disintegrating Commonwealth.

The whites in South West Africa have nothing to fear from London, Paris, or the duplicity displayed by these capitals in recent years. Pretoria is behind them, and its interests coincide with theirs. The threat and the danger may only come from the United Nations. But a United Nations intervention is a far more complicated affair than was the Algerian precedent where matters were settled from and by Paris.

The opposition in Windhoek maintains that the South West African white community is about equally divided between their desire to join the Republic, and the other inclination to become eventually independent in a United Nations–sponsored arrangement. This assumption is absolutely groundless. The whites in South West Africa know exactly with which side the United Nations aligns itself. This has been amply demonstrated during the last fifteen years. A United Nations–sponsored independence would result, just as it did in New Guinea, in an entirely black (majority) regime, since the United Nations, in systematic contempt of realities, is determined to drive through, wherever it has the power to do so, the principle of "one man, one vote." A few years after such independence, the South West African whites would be compelled to leave, and even be accused of refusal to cooperate.

The truth is, and anybody can hear it for himself up and down the territory, that almost all whites, including the voters for the opposition, loyally support the government in its overall policies in regard to South West Africa, whether at the United Nations or at The Hague. Economically, they owe Pretoria the fact that the balance of payments remains favorable, and the taxes remain low.

The situation in this respect resembles that of Alaska before it became a state; but just as Alaska finally voted for statehood, so the South Westers would also vote for incorporation as the Republic's fifth province,* in case of pressure or attack from outside.

The same argument holds when we hear the opposition intellectuals' wishful thinking that the German-speaking population insists on retaining the specificity of South West Africa, and not let it dissolve in the framework of the Republic. But in spite of my careful inquiries, I was unable to detect the slightest signs of a separate "German" thinking or interest. All white men in South West Africa are in the same boat, and would be kicked out of the boat if the United Nations were allowed to meddle.

We witnessed already in the case of Rhodesia that London's hands are not long enough to bring down the independence-minded regime and break the will of the population. The distances are too long, Rhodesia's neighbors are helping her, and most of all, London is well aware that military intervention would spark endless violence and warfare in southern and central Africa, engulfing everything, including the heavy British investments in those parts of the world.

These arguments hold with regard to South West Africa also. The latter is much less industrialized even than Rhodesia, and its trade with the outside world is also much less extensive. It simply cannot be hurt unless South Africa is hurt first, or at the same time. But this would be

* The other four are Cape, Orange Free State, Transvaal, and Natal.

a *casus belli,* with the same bloody consequences as an offensive against Rhodesia. Furthermore, while Rhodesia's frontiers are open to the north (on the Zambian side), South West Africa is protected by Portuguese Angola. In fact, it is the link between the Portuguese and the South Africans. Its loss or even chaos on the territory is something that neither the Portuguese nor Pretoria can tolerate.

There remains the question of a United Nations intervention. If a similar intervention proved disastrous and futile in the Congo and Katanga (1961–63) it is unlikely that the new attempt would be made in an even more distant and inimical territory. Besides, behind the Congo intervention there were also the interests of international finance and of the world's big copper producers. South West Africa is simply not rich and successful enough to make an attack against it worthwhile for the gentlemen in the United Nations, who like to combine the cheap glory of sentimental slogans with other more material benefits. In short, an already bankrupt United Nations would think twice before embarking on such an essentially barren operation.

This does not mean at all that the possibility of such an intervention must be excluded. Precisely because it is declining a United Nations majority might decide to re-varnish its fading reputation and launch an attack in the name of this or that. "Decide" of course is a big word when used in reference to the United Nations; rather its chief sponsor and paymaster, Washington, will have to decide, and it would not be Washington's first suicidal choice. It is to be hoped, however, that at least some American diplomats and Presidential advisors know who the adversary would be: South Africa. So let us speak now the language of reality, nothing but the language of reality, concerning this country.

South Africa today is an expanding country, not in terms of foreign conquests, but as a healthy, vigorous young nation, flexing its muscles, and discovering, to its own astonishment, how much it can achieve. One of these achievements is that in twenty years, this mainly agricultural land has become one of the world's fifteen most important industrial countries. The other, no less important, achievement is something that words cannot express: a moral vigor, an undivided loyalty to a cause which may appear annoying to the superficial observer, but which reveals the fibers of which great nations and great enterprises are woven. In the western world, as far as I can see, there are only three such nations possessing this "stuff": the Americans, the Portuguese, and the South Africans.

The expansionism of the South Africans requires the large field of activity that is Southern Africa. Whether in the form of a system of economic cooperation, or in some other form, South Africa, together with the black and white states of the subcontinent, will organize this enormous and enormously promising territory for the benefit of all. South West Africa is part of it and on account of its relative poverty and underpopulation, it needs the others and the others need it. It is absolutely inconceivable that Pretoria would ever renounce the vast territory to the north at a time when the country is expanding, not shrink-

ing. A blow of that kind and magnitude would destroy
South African morale, creative power, and possibility of
further kneading the material called Africa. Such setbacks
in midcourse do not happen; just as the United States
could not be stopped by all the power in the world from
reaching in its westward expansion the Pacific Ocean.

Thus the most realistic way for Americans to view what
is now happening in South Africa is to look at it as
propelled by a "manifest destiny." Each nation has it once
in its existence as a kind of divine dowry: Athens had it,
and the Romans, the Spanish, the French, the Portuguese,
the British, the Dutch, the Russians. The South Africans
also have it: now! And it would be naive to imagine that
their manifest destiny would be fulfilled by securing
South West Africa only. The second thrust after the
consolidation of southern Africa will be in northerly direction, perhaps fifteen or twenty years hence. By that
time the passions of *uhuru* will have subsided and Africa
will not be a novelty for Washington and Moscow, but
rather an annoying economic burden. Then will the South
Africans come forward, as they must with a "Marshall
Plan" of their own, aiding Africa and healing its many
wounds.

Meanwhile, South West Africa will be defended by
force of arms if necessary. Nobody told me this in Windhoek, Capetown, or Pretoria, and I did not expect anybody to tell me. Yet it is clear. The respected moderate ex-
Rhodesian Prime Minister, Sir Edgar Whitehead, wrote
recently in a British periodical that if Rhodesia falls,
Mozambique cannot stand, and the encouraged African

nationalists' next offensive would be directed at South West Africa through the United Nations. The new pretext would be that South West Africa had been granted as a mandate to the British Crown; if London had the right to act against Rhodesia, it would have to act according to what would be then construed as logic in favor of majority rule in South West Africa, too. At any rate, the consequences are incalculable, but bloodshed would not be avoided.

Whether under these circumstances, or even before, South Africa would annex South West Africa, cannot be foretold. But two things are certain. Even if the World Court renders a judgment favorable to South Africa, the latter's enemies in Africa and the United Nations will not disarm. They would only respect the verdict if it is favorable to them. If not, they will simply mount new offensives. The other thing which is sure is that if South Africa yields to black nationalism then not only its whole policy of apartheid collapses, but it also signs its own death sentence as a nation.

There appears to be no way out of the dilemma. My own conviction is that South Africa will overcome the difficulties which now assail it. This constitutes the best hope for South West Africa and its entire population.

APPENDIX

MANDATE FOR GERMAN SOUTH WEST AFRICA

The Council of the League of Nations:

Whereas by Article 119 of the Treaty of Peace with Germany signed at Versailles on June 28th, 1919, Germany renounced in favor of the Principal Allied and Associated Powers all her rights over her overseas possessions, including therein German South-West Africa; and

Whereas the Principal Allied and Associated Powers agreed that, in accordance with Article 22 Part I (Covenant of the League of Nations) of the said Treaty, a Mandate should be conferred upon His Britannic Majesty to be exercised on his behalf by the Government of the Union of South Africa to administer the territory aforementioned, and have proposed that the Mandate should be formulated in the following terms; and

Whereas His Britannic Majesty, for and on behalf of the Government of the Union of South Africa, has agreed to accept the Mandate in respect of the said territory and has undertaken to exercise it on behalf of the League of Nations in accordance with the following provisions; and

Whereas, by the aforementioned Article 22, paragraph 8, it is provided that the degree of authority, control or administration to be exercised by the Mandatory not previously agreed upon by the Members of the League, shall be explicitly defined by the Council of the League of Nations:

Confirming the said Mandate, defines its terms as follows:

ARTICLE 1. The territory over which a Mandate is conferred upon His Britannic Majesty for and on behalf of the Government of the Union of South Africa (hereinafter called the Mandatory) comprises the territory which formerly constituted the German Protectorate of South-West Africa.

ARTICLE 2. The Mandatory shall have full power of administration and legislation over the territory subject to the present Mandate as an integral portion of the Union of South Africa, and may apply the laws of the Union of South Africa to the territory, subject to such local modifications as circumstances may require.

The Mandatory shall promote to the utmost the material and moral well-being and the social progress of the inhabitants of the territory subject to the present Mandate.

ARTICLE 3.   The Mandatory shall see that the slave trade is prohibited, and that no forced labour is permitted, except for essential public works and services, and then only for adequate renumeration.

The Mandatory shall also see that the traffic in arms and ammunition is controlled in accordance with principles analogous to those laid down in the Convention relating to the control of the arms traffic, signed on September 10th, 1919, or in any convention amending the same.

The supply of intoxicating spirits and beverages to the natives shall be prohibited.

ARTICLE 4.   The military training of the natives, otherwise than for purposes of internal police and the local defence of the territory, shall be prohibited. Furthermore, no military or naval bases shall be established or fortifications erected in the territory.

ARTICLE 5.   Subject to the provisions of any local law for the maintenance of public morals, the Mandatory shall ensure in the territory freedom of conscience and the free exercise of all forms of worship, and shall allow all missionaries, nationals or any State Member of the League of Nations, to enter into, travel and reside in the territory for the purpose of prosecuting their calling.

ARTICLE 6.   The Mandatory shall make to the Council of the League of Nations an annual report to the satisfaction of the Council, containing full information with regard to the territory, and indicating the measures taken to carry out the obligations assumed under Articles 2, 3, 4 and 5.

ARTICLE 7.   The consent of the Council of the League of Nations is required for any modification of the terms of the present Mandate.

The Mandatory agrees that, if any dispute whatever should arise between the Mandatory and another Member of the League of Nations relating to the interpretation or the application of the provisions of the Mandate, such dispute, if it cannot be settled by negotiation, shall be submitted to the Permanent Court of International Justice provided for by Article 14 of the Covenant of the League of Nations.

The present Declaration shall be deposited in the archives of the League of Nations. Certified copies shall be forwarded by the Secretary-General of the League of Nations to all Powers Signatories of the Treaty of Peace with Germany.

Made at Geneva the 17th day of December, 1920.

Extracts from Summary of Decision of
International Court of Justice in the Case of South West Africa
Made Public July 18, 1966

The International Court of Justice today delivered its judgment in the second phase of the South-West Africa cases (Ethiopia v. South Africa, Liberia v. South Africa).

These cases, relating to the continued existence of the mandate for South-West Africa and the duties and performance of South Africa as mandatory thereunder, were instituted by applications of the Governments of Ethiopia and Liberia filed in the registry of 4 November 1960. By an order of 20 May 1961 the Court joined the proceedings in the two cases. The Government of South Africa raised preliminary objections to the Court's proceeding to hear the merits of the case but these were dismissed by the Court on 21 December 1962, the Court finding that it had jurisdiction to adjudicate upon the merits of the dispute.

In its judgment delivered today, the Court began by recalling that the applicants, acting in the capacity of states which were members of the former League of Nations, put forward various allegations of contraventions of the League of Nations mandate for South-West Africa by the Republic of South Africa.

The contentions of the parties covered inter alia the following issues: Whether the mandate for South-West Africa was still in force and if so whether the mandatory's obligation to furnish annual reports on its administration to the Council of the League of Nations had become transformed into an obligation so to report to the General Assembly of the United Nations; whether the respondent had in accordance with the mandate promoted to the utmost the material and moral well-being and the social progress of the inhabitants of the territory; whether the mandatory had contravened the prohibition in the mandate of the "military training of the natives" and the establishment of military or naval bases or the erection of fortifications in the territory and whether South Africa had contravened the provision in the mandate that it can only be modified with the consent of the Council of the League of Nations by attempting to modify the mandate without the consent of the United Nations General Assembly which, it was contended by the applicants, had replaced the Council of the League for this and other purposes.

Before dealing with these questions, however, the Court considered that there were two questions of an antecedent character appertaining to the merits of the case, which might render an inquiry into other aspects of the case unnecessary. One was whether the mandate still subsisted at all, and the other was the question of the applicants' standing in this phase of the proceedings—i.e., their legal right or interest regarding the subject matter of their claims.

As the court based its judgment on a finding that the applicants did not possess such a legal right or interest, it did not pronounce upon the question of whether the mandate was still in force. Moreover, the Court emphasized that its 1962 decision on the question of competence was given without prejudice to the question of the survival of the mandate—a question appertaining to the merits of the case, and not in issue in 1962 except in the sense that survival had to be assumed for the purpose of determining the purely jurisdictional issue which was all that was then before the Court.

(*The court then gives an analysis of its reasoning in the case.*)

For the foregoing reasons, the Court, by the President's casting vote, the votes being equally divided (seven–seven), found that Ethiopia and Liberia could not be considered to have established any legal right or interest in the subject matter of their claims, and, accordingly, decided to reject them.